THE TEACH YOURSELF BOOKS

CATERING
AND HOTEL MANAGEMENT

TEACH YOURSELF
CATERING
AND
HOTEL MANAGEMENT

V. G. WINSLET
A.S.A.A., A.C.I.S.

THE ENGLISH UNIVERSITIES PRESS LTD
ST. PAUL'S HOUSE   WARWICK LANE
LONDON EC4

The publishers are indebted to Mr Clifford Witting for his
assistance in preparing this book for publication and to
Mr R. O. Baker for revising this impression.

First printed 1955
This impression 1968

S.B.N. 340 05541 3

*Printed in Great Britain for the English Universities Press Ltd.,
by Richard Clay (The Chaucer Press), Ltd., Bungay, Suffolk*

INTRODUCTION

On those engaged in the top-level range of the catering industry the demands made are numerous and heavy, and possibly no other vocation makes such inroads into a man's private time and life. To anyone who is willing to accept such conditions it provides compensations and sometimes rich rewards, not all of a material kind.

Some of the attributes required are good health, unlimited patience, tact, a placid temperament, a lively interest in people and things, the capacity to meet emergencies, solve them quickly and originate action, and a wide practical experience in every aspect of the industry, with the ability to direct every employee in his job and enforce discipline with the inflexibility of a sergeant-major mellowed by the benevolence of a humane magistrate.

The success of any establishment rests very largely on the staff employed. If the industry is to be efficient in every respect, there is no room for wasted effort due to misplaced labour, with its consequent frustration and unhappiness. From personnel, as from proprietors, the industry demands initiative, really hard work, together with high standards of cleanliness, of buying, preparing and presenting food, and of everything that goes to give *service* in its widest and best sense to the community at large. It is not a matter of serving a cup of coffee or a six-course dinner, but of selling a specialized product allied with the personal service of everyone engaged in the industry.

Despite the impetus of mass production as a dominant factor in our lives to-day, there still remains scope for individual expression. One source is where a person, usually a lady, opens a small tea-room or café in a seaside or country resort. This is a grand opportunity to reflect individuality by furnishing and equipping to personal taste. But there are pitfalls, and it is to guide the unwary away from these that this textbook has been written.

Herein are set out as fully as possible the salient facts relating to the catering industry in general and its daily operation. The author has had many years of the closest contact with its varied demands, its often exciting incidents, and its absorbing interests. He hopes sincerely that the knowledge imparted will be of value to all readers, whether they have attained executive positions, are about to set up in some catering enterprise, or presently occupy quite humble places in this great industry.

CONTENTS

CHAPTER I

**Growth of the Catering Industry—Inns and Hotels—
Places of Refreshment—The Hotel and Catering Institute
—Principal Trade Organizations**

GROWTH OF THE CATERING INDUSTRY

THE catering industry in this country to-day employs over
750,000 persons at its peak season, and occupies fourth
place in our national industries. Its history goes back to
Biblical times, when the necessity and urge to travel,
either on foot or by mule, camel or horse, led to the
setting up of places where rest and refreshment for man
and beast could be obtained. Down the long corridors
of time, inns have played a large part in the national life of
almost every civilized community; in our own country
alone there are scores of names of inns that have featured
in our chronicles and literature.

During the last forty years great strides have been
made. Enterprise, backed by the necessary capital and
energy, has so extended the scope of the catering industry
that its services, once the almost exclusive privilege of the
wealthy classes, are now easily available to nearly everyone.
All over the country are well-planned, attractively decorated and furnished premises in which refreshment of
every type and price can be obtained. Wherever people
congregate for business or pleasure, wherever they may
travel and by whatever means, the industry is represented
in some form: inns, hotels, boarding-houses, guest-houses,
restaurants, tea-rooms, cafés, snack-bars, canteens. In air
liners one can partake of a sumptuous meal complete with
appropriate wines, while packed snacks and beverages are
procurable in many of our long-distance motor-coaches.

Despite immense difficulties there has been steady growth
in the manufacture by firms of repute of a great range of
high-class plant, equipment and utensils. In keeping with

existing labour difficulties, much of their effort has been directed towards effecting saving of labour, time and money. With the end of food rationing, hotels and restaurants were able to return to normal, and healthy competition was re-established. In the past five years there has been enormous development, particularly in the field of popular catering, and new hotels and restaurants are being opened in all parts of the country.

INNS AND HOTELS

The law in general regarding hotels and inns is contained in the Hotel Proprietors Act, 1957, which has superseded the Innkeepers Liability Act, 1863. This new Act retains the old English legal word " inn ", but gives, for the first time, a legal definition of a hotel and says, in effect, that the only type of premises which are to be " inns " in the legal sense are hotels. A hotel is defined in the Act as " an establishment held out by the proprietor as offering food, drink and, if so required, sleeping accommodation, without special contract, to any traveller presenting himself who appears able and willing to pay a reasonable sum for the services and facilities provided and who is in a fit state to be received ".

This definition of a " hotel ", and therefore an " inn ", is somewhat the same as under the former law, but differs in two important features. To be an " inn " a hotel must have sleeping accommodation on offer, and any accommodation, food or drink offered must be available " without special contract ", i.e., without terms having been arranged beforehand.

In other words, if a hotel holds itself out as available to provide bed and board for any chance customer, it is an " inn " and becomes subject to the various rights, duties and obligations of an innkeeper. No other premises are " inns " in the legal sense.

The proprietors of inns as defined have the obligation to receive travellers (whether for food, drink or sleeping), and the right of retention and sale of luggage if the guest cannot pay his bill. They also have liabilities as to the safety of a guest's goods.

First, an innkeeper, like everyone else, is fully liable for the total amount of loss or damage caused by his own default, negligence or wilful act, or of that of his staff. But his special liability as innkeeper goes beyond this, and makes him responsible for loss and damage even if he is not at fault in any way.

This special innkeeper's liability applies only in respect of guests for whom sleeping accommodation has been booked, and only then when the loss or damage occurs between the midnight before arrival and the midnight after departure of the guest.

The " traveller " who drops in for a drink or a meal is no longer (as he could under the former law) able to claim for loss or damage to his goods, unless it is due to the fault of the innkeeper or his staff.

The Act makes a special exception for any vehicle or property left therein, or any horse, animal or harness or equipment. The special liability of an innkeeper does not apply to these things; nor has he any lien or right of retention over these things.

Where an innkeeper is liable, as innkeeper, for loss or damage, this special liability can be limited to £50 for any one article, and £100 in total for any one guest. To get the benefit of this limitation, a specified form of notice must be displayed on the premises. Wording for these notices, which must be displayed at or near the reception desk or main entrance, is given in the Act. This limitation of liability does not apply where property is deposited for safe custody with the innkeeper; or has been offered for deposit and been refused.

Proprietors of boarding- and guest-houses and private

hotels (as distinct from inns) are not generally liable for loss of guests' property, unless negligence is proved; nor can they exercise a lien on guests' property against an unpaid bill.

The bringing into the establishment of dogs or other animals is very often a matter of dispute, but the innkeeper can generally refuse to allow them in the public rooms. Accommodation is often provided in kennels and out-houses.

Although the primary service of the hotel is to provide food and shelter for such periods as patrons may desire and require, other important auxiliary services have been added in modern times. Practically all such establishments are open to non-residents and anyone can have a meal in the dining-room or restaurant, partake of a drink at one of the bars or in one of the lounges, or avail himself of the many other forms of service offered. Mention may be made of such facilities as: laundry, cleaning, pressing and valet services; booking of seats at places of entertainment or for travel by rail, sea, air and road; car hire; hairdressing and beauty parlours; telephone; kiosks for the sale of confections, cigarettes, toilet preparations, pharmaceutical supplies, newspapers, magazines, stationery, etc. Hotels are also available for functions or banquets of every nature, as well as for conferences, business meetings, annual general meetings and the like.

A new factor in the British hotel industry in recent years has been the development of motels—inns specially designed for motorists. Some forty motels have been opened on or near main highways and are proving popular and successful. Motorists appreciate them for their reasonable tariffs, lack of formality and ease of access. It seems certain that the present number of motels (January 1963) will be at least doubled within the next five years.

PLACES OF REFRESHMENT

The proprietor of a restaurant, tea-room, etc., has the liberty of refusing to serve anyone, and he has no responsibility for patrons' property. In nearly all establishments of this class printed notices to this effect are prominently displayed. In one respect the proprietor may incur liability, and that is when he provides a cloak-room with a member of his staff in charge of it. If the patron leaves his overcoat, hat, etc. and receives in exchange a numbered ticket, he is entitled to have his property returned intact on production of the ticket.

Save for the large increase in canteens during and since World War II, there has been no greater development in the catering industry than that arising from the advent of the cafeteria, the restaurant in which the customer serves himself. Two factors helped to bring this about: the rapid rise in running costs, especially on the labour side; and the vast increase in the number of persons who now eat out and who demand speedy service. During the past decade the increase in these self-service establishments throughout the country has been remarkable. The patron can select or reject as he pleases dishes (either hot or cold) from displays set out in various ways on a service counter. Tea, coffee and soft drinks are similarly available. The patron knows the exact cost of each dish, and at the end of the service counter the cashier requests payment for whatever food and beverages are on the tray. The patron then settles himself at a table, consumes his repast, then leaves the cafeteria without having to tip a waitress or wait for her to supply him with a check.

While turnover is largely dictated by the degree of excellence of display, salesmanship of the silent variety can be most effective in this type of enterprise. To achieve a high degree of success, the organization required differs from that for a restaurant or tea-room in that supplies and replenishments must be quickly available. A close liaison must exist between kitchen, service-room and counter, so that supplies are forthcoming as and when required. The supply of beverages is highly important, for much valuable goodwill can be built up by consistently serving an excellent cup of tea or coffee.

Snack-bars and milk-bars differ from the cafeteria in that cash is usually paid direct to the assistant serving the patron with his beverage and food. The two establishments are somewhat similar to each other, the milk-bar probably being a little older in origin, having begun as a speedy purveyor of milk in various forms—hot, cold, milk-shake, sundaes, etc. To-day it is virtually a snack-bar, serving tea, coffee, soft drinks, sandwiches (bread and rolls) with fillings of many varieties, pastries, etc. Stools are provided at the serving counter, on which are displayed the provisions for sale. Other patrons may stand around, placing their cups on shelves, as space usually limits the number of tables supplied, and in any case these are small.

It would be well-nigh impossible to measure how much is due to canteens for the splendid war effort made by our people during the trying years of 1939 to 1945. The service given by industrial canteens in providing all workers and staff with well-cooked meals served in often comfortable surroundings for the twenty-four hours of every day is one that should never be forgotten. Those long years of travail by bombing, black-out, food rationing and general anxiety were immeasurably lightened by these canteens and by all those who faithfully worked therein.

These important adjuncts to present-day industry and commerce have several peculiar features that require a somewhat different form of organization from the accepted basis of ordinary catering ventures. Intensive planning is required to ensure extremely rapid service at all peak periods, staff being organized in such a way as to avoid any risk of breakdown of service at any point. There must be diplomatic treatment of all complaints and suggestions that may and do emanate from the workers through canteen committees and other channels. Where a night shift is worked it raises problems of preparation and service of meals, collection of cash or tickets, and it so often leads to extensive pilfering. Where service is made available during most of the twenty-four hours, it is necessary to work on the shift system.

In the main the same principles apply to canteens as to all other catering establishments, so far as the day-to-day routine is concerned. Purchasing and care of food, its preparation and presentation are equally important.

It is generally found that the cafeteria system is popular in canteens, but where the numbers to be served are large, the multi-point system is effective. Long queues whose pace is often dictated by the indecision of one individual are broken up into several sections in the multi-point system. The workers are informed by means of large menu boards what is available and the price, and go to the respective serving points. Here nothing is on display, service of main course, sweets and sundries being given through windows or hatches. Payment must be made either with the exact amount in cash or by ticket of appropriate value, no change being given. This system is admirable where speed of service is essential, but it involves pre-plating on an extensive scale. Provided circumstances permit, the cafeteria system is preferable.

Progress has also been made in the adoption of automatic food vending machines, particularly for hot and cold drinks, snacks and sandwiches in industrial canteens during late night shifts. Attempts to use vending machines to supply complete hot meals have not so far been received with much enthusiasm by workers.

THE HOTEL AND CATERING INSTITUTE

Incorporated in 1949, this is the professional body of the catering industry and its official organization for the development of hotel and catering education. The headquarters are at 24 Portman Square, London, W.1 (Telephone: Welbeck 6554–7). The principal trade associations are represented on the council, while many Ministries, Government departments and other official bodies are represented on the education committee by assessors, liaison officers and observers.

PRINCIPAL TRADE ORGANIZATIONS

British Hotels and Restaurants Association, 88 Brook Street, London, W.1. (Telephone: Grosvenor 6641.)

Caterers' Association of Great Britain, Victoria House, Vernon Place, Southampton Row, London, W.C.1. (Telephone: Holborn 1795.)

Industrial Catering Association, 53/54 King William Street, London, E.C.4. (Telephone: Mincing Lane 9143.)

Cookery and Food Association, 185 Piccadilly, London, W.1. (Telephone: Regent 2460.)

Hospital Caterers' Association, 54 Lyford Road, Wandsworth, London, S.W.18. (Telephone: Vandyke 8326.)

British Federation of Hotel and Boarding House Associations, 33 Birley Street, Blackpool, Lancs. (Telephone: Blackpool 24241.)

National Trade Development Association, 42 Portman Square, London W.1. (Telephone: Welbeck 0382.)

Wine and Spirit Association of Great Britain, 1 Vintners Place, Upper Thames Street, London, E.C.4. (Telephone: City 5377.)

National Caterers' Federation, 156 Camden High Street, London, N.W.1. (Telephone: Gulliver 7060.)

CHAPTER II

Taking Over a Going Concern—Opening a New Business—Purchasing the Premises—Mortgages—Insurances—Life Assurance—Precautions Against Fire—Powers of Local Authorities—Income Tax

TAKING OVER A GOING CONCERN

THIS chapter opens with a word of warning. It is of vital importance that everyone entering or proposing to enter the catering industry should have had previous practical experience in some branch. Without it any venture is likely to be doomed to failure.

When contemplating the purchase of a going concern, be it a hotel, restaurant, tea-room, snack-bar or cafeteria, the first consideration must be location. Individual preference may exist—a busy market town, perhaps, or a seaside resort or an industrial city—but whatever the choice, the prospective purchaser should satisfy himself on certain points before passing his word to buy. Consideration must be given to:—

1. The type of human activity in the neighbourhood, e.g. industrial, general trading, farming or resort. Is future expansion anticipated, or is the situation static? If a resort, what is the length of the season? Some places experience ten weeks only of hectic business, others have much longer at a more steady pace, while a few are fortunate enough to have the whole year. If an industrial area, is it subject to fluctuations according to the state of the local industries? Future prospects are important. Is the locality dependent on a number of industries or confined to one or two only? If one or two only, a recession may prove harmful.

2. The type and number of competitors, the general

17

condition of existing establishments, and the positions occupied.

3. The type and general character of the population. Is it increasing? What is the income level?

4. Is the local government progressive? Are the public services well managed?

Various other factors are:—

5. Is the intending caterer well known in the town or locality?

6. Are the potential patrons of his particular type?

7. Is the local population likely to eat out in sufficient numbers? If in a city area, will trade be limited to a busy luncheon period, or will it be a steady all-day trade supplemented by a good evening trade to make the proposition worth while?

A good plan is to pay visits to the existing establishments in the town or district preferred and note carefully the number and type of patrons, the style of fittings, the table appointments, the menu, the size of portions, the standard of cooking and presentation. In industrial districts size of portion is primarily the deciding factor for success, while in residential districts variety of dishes, comfort and pleasant surroundings are desired.

Positions near rail and bus stations and places of entertainment are usually good, as are often large parking centres. It is wise to keep clear of schools and churches.

Before purchasing a business, make a thorough investigation into the state of it. Engage the services of a professional accountant to examine the financial books, and a surveyor to make a report on the condition of the premises.

Points requiring attention are:—

1. Number of years that the business has been established.

2. Whether the premises are freehold or leasehold.

If leasehold, ascertain: (*a*) length of unexpired period; (*b*) rent payable and if any increases are contemplated; (*c*) dates when rent falls due to be paid; (*d*) position relating to external and internal repairs; (*e*) if structural alterations would be permitted; (*f*) estimate of annual cost of repairs and renewals; (*g*) if lease can be renewed and on what terms; (*h*) if there are any special conditions.

3. Rateable valuations.

4. Whether the district is liable to depreciate.

5. If a shopping or amusement centre, how any material change would affect business.

6. Whether the local services of gas, electricity and water are adequate.

Close scrutiny must be made of a comparative statement prepared by the accountant. It should cover a period of, say, five years and should show among other items: turnover suitably analysed; purchases; gross profits; detailed expense items such as rent, rates, heating, lighting, power, wages, national insurance, publicity, printing and stationery, insurances; value and condition of stock in hand; value placed on plant, equipment, fittings, fixtures, loose utensils, furniture, linen, china, glass and cutlery.

Every item of expense should be carefully checked and the percentages compared one year with another. Note particularly the sums spent on renewals of equipment, china, glass, etc., as well as on general upkeep. A marked decrease on all or any of these items during the latter years might conceivably point to severe retrenchment, having in mind an early sale. It must, however, be borne in mind when studying these figures that all costs have risen rapidly during the past decade. Again, the spending power of the general public has decreased in some directions, and, with the increased quantity and quality now available, they are becoming much more discriminating.

The price for the goodwill is usually based on the average of the net profits for 3–5 years multiplied by the number of years taken into the calculation.

Labour is important. Ascertain whether the present staff is likely to remain under the new régime, and whether those available are trained, semi-trained, untrained or mere daily helps.

Keep in mind the insertion of a restraint-of-trade clause in the final agreement, in order to guard against unfair competition from the present owner or manager. Keep in mind too the possibility of future extension, and tactfully inquire the position regarding additions to the present building, and the views of owners of adjoining property.

Should your choice be a holiday resort, ascertain if the local government is really exerting itself to keep the resort up to date and attractive. Read over the town's advertising and the local brochure.

Finally, does your choice appear to have the merit of being efficiently and easily worked?

OPENING A NEW BUSINESS

Here extreme caution must be exercised, for property purchased at a low price frequently involves such expenditure on conversion that the final result is costly. Employ a surveyor or architect to examine the building thoroughly and advise just how much alteration is required and how much it will cost. Ease of service is vital. Better a long two-storey building than a smaller four-storey building involving the heavy expense of installing a lift. Endeavour to have the kitchen, service-room and dining-room on one level. The provision of toilets and bathrooms can also prove an expensive matter.

Do the available bedrooms lend themselves to provide

a fair proportion of single and double rooms? Is there space for a garage or parking site? Is there a flower-garden and lawn? Is there space for a vegetable garden? This is a good advertising point, and the produce therefrom is a welcome addition to the kitchen operations.

These are some of the pertinent questions one must ask oneself, and unless satisfactory answers to all or most of them can be obtained, it is better to continue the search elsewhere.

In a seaside resort, a position on the front or esplanade is usually well worth the extra cost. Remember to inquire as to the length of season.

Should the desire be for a restaurant, tea-room, etc., much of what has already been written applies. Weigh up every factor before deciding, as it is much easier to go in than to come out. Sometimes the opening of a restaurant or tea-room of an unusual type or design achieves considerable success, but whether this degree of prosperity is permanent is a matter for conjecture, for the public are extremely fickle.

Easy working is an important factor, and may well save the wages of a couple of employees, with food in addition. Accessibility is another point; petrol rationing and shortage caused severe loss to many establishments in the war and early post-war years. Consider the question of supplies. Distance from a town and consequent transport difficulties may entail buying larger quantities, thus locking up capital that could possibly be more profitably employed in some other way.

PURCHASING THE PREMISES

If the premises are freehold the transaction is governed by the law of contract, whereby an offer is made by the purchaser, which is " subject to contract ", and a deposit of ten per cent is paid. Should the vendor be agreeable, a formal contract is drawn up, which, once signed, is binding on both parties. If the purchaser withdraws, he cannot demand repayment of his deposit, but if the vendor withdraws, the purchaser can reclaim his deposit. Despite the fact that the contract does not transfer the legal ownership of the property to the purchaser, he is looked upon as the owner and should take immediate steps to insure the property against all fire risks. The whole matter is usually concluded at a later date by the execution of a conveyance and the handing over of the relative title-deeds.

If the premises are leasehold a lease for a specified number of years is purchased on payment of a round sum plus an annual ground rent. The terms of a lease vary from a few years to 999 years, which latter term is practically a freehold. Terms exceeding three years must be by deed. A leaseholder may himself rent the property thus leased to another party, giving him a proportionately shorter period. For example, the original leaseholder may have a ninety-nine years' lease and be willing to grant an underlease for, say, twenty-one years, with the option to renew for a further period of twenty-one years if the parties are in full agreement.

The detailed terms of any lease form the basis of the agreement between the lessor and the lessee. These include among other matters: full names and addresses of the parties; full address and description of the premises to be leased; term of the lease with dates; amount of rent payable and dates of payment thereof, a time limit being usually stated to promote prompt payment; which party is to pay general and water rates; clauses relating to internal and external repairs, painting, etc., and periodic inspection of the premises; any rules and regulations relating to the general care and well-being of the property; option to renew, and the rent to be payable; and possibly an arbitration clause in the event of any disputes arising. These are the main points, but many leases are extremely fully worded, and close reading is essential to extract the wheat from the chaff.

MORTGAGES

Should the purchaser of a freehold or a leasehold find that he is likely to be short of funds to meet the whole of the purchase price, it is customary to borrow the required sum on mortgage. When this deal has been completed the lender (mortgagee) has in his possession the mortgage deed and also the title-deeds of the property. The borrower (mortgagor) agrees to pay interest on the sum advanced at an agreed rate and on stated dates. Many mortgages are repayable in 15–20 years by payments made either quarterly or half-yearly. These payments comprise interest on the sum advanced and an instalment of the capital. Although the sum paid each year remains static, as time passes the proportion in name of interest decreases and the sum in repayment of the principal sum increases.

INSURANCES

Generally speaking, insurance is a contract of indemnity made between two parties, whereby the insured party, upon payment, usually annually, to the insurer of a sum of money, called the premium, agrees to such measure of indemnification as may be set out in the contract, evidenced by the policy. Anyone may insure, provided he possesses an insurable interest in the subject matter, e.g. buildings, plant, stock, etc. It is imperative that *all* material facts be disclosed when the proposal is made, as any failure to give the fullest information can easily invalidate the contract.

A caterer should insure against the following risks: fire, burglary, employer's liability, motor, engineering, third party, fidelity, plate glass, loss of licence, action for food poisoning, loss of profits.

Fire.—This policy should adequately cover the present-day value of the building (if owned) and all contents. Frequently such a policy is extended to cover such additional risks as explosion (other than that of domestic boilers, which are usually included in the fire policy), storm, flood and tempest; bursting or overflowing of cisterns, water-pipes, etc.; aircraft and/or articles dropped therefrom; riot, civil commotion, strikes and others involved in labour disturbances; earthquakes; damage by any road vehicle, etc. A fire policy may be (*a*) specific or (*b*) average. The first insures for a fixed sum payable if the actual loss reaches that amount, regardless of the actual value of the property insured. The second is fairly common, its effect being to make the insured bear a proportion of the loss. If, for instance, property is insured for £500, but its actual value is £1,000, then in the event of a total loss, the insurer pays to the insured the sum of £250, being half of the loss, on the assumption that the insured bears responsibility for the balance.

Burglary.—This risk is ever present, and while it can be fully insured, it is the responsibility of the owner to ensure that every care is taken by providing necessary locks, etc. and efficient window-fastening.

Employer's Liability.—Whilst the National Insurance (Industrial Injuries) Act, 1946, which came into force on 5th July 1948, relieves employers of liability under the Workmen's Compensation Act for accidents, employees still retain the right under common law to raise a claim for damages, and if the accident proves fatal, a claim may be brought by the dependants of the deceased under the Fatal Accident Act, 1846. Employers are also liable for damages for any accident caused by fellow employees. As recent awards in courts have been substantial, adequate cover is advised. Employer's liability and national insurance are dealt with more fully in Chapter V.

Motor.—Under the Road Traffic Act the driver of every

vehicle must be insured against the risk of causing death or bodily injury to any person. Cover should also be taken against damage to or loss of the vehicle, injuries sustained by the insured, loss of luggage, etc.

Engineering.—This policy should cover loss or damage due to breakdown of lifts, boilers, refrigerators, etc., injury to employees, and loss of life. It may also include a breakdown insurance.

Third Party.—This risk is highly important and must be covered. Accidents to patrons may happen at any time; they may slip on polished floors; a worn carpet or faulty stair-rod may cause them to fall downstairs. Cover should include the cost of legal action, especially defending extravagant claims.

Fidelity.—The risk of defalcation by staff is unfortunately ever present and must be fully covered. The insurance company investigates the history of every employee accepted by them, so an employer can place full reliance on such employees.

Plate Glass.—This should cover all windows, glass doors, etc.

Loss of Licence.—This is extremely important to the holder of a liquor licence, for its loss would prove highly detrimental to the business.

Food Poisoning.—Despite every care, accidents do happen, and the cost to the caterer can be exceptionally heavy.

Loss of Profits.—Some owners may consider that the premium paid is warranted by the damage that might result from fire, etc. preventing the business from functioning.

LIFE ASSURANCE

This is not a contract of indemnity, but one whereby the insured, on payment of the agreed premium, receives from the insurer a sum on his attaining a certain age, or it may be on death. Premiums may be single payments or, as is more usual, annual. Premiums on fixed policies are lower than those on policies with profits.

For the small owner a life policy is beneficial, for these reasons: on maturity or at death it provides a much-needed sum of money; it is a form of compulsory saving; income-tax allowance is given on a certain portion of the premium paid; it provides an acceptable form of security for a bank overdraft. The value is usually based on what is known as the surrender value, which is the sum the insurance company is prepared to pay for immediate cancellation of the policy.

PRECAUTIONS AGAINST FIRE

As in all classes of business enterprise, an outbreak of fire, a minor explosion or similar happening may lead to decline of trade while the necessary repairs and replacement of equipment are being carried out. All this loss may not be fully covered by insurance, and in addition there must be considered the effect of shock upon patrons, guests and staff.

Ascertain, therefore, that the premises do not contain any structural or other fittings, fixtures, etc. that might create a fire hazard. Have the electrical installation inspected at intervals. Make certain that the risk from fat, etc. boiling over is minimized; that fish-fryers are adequately hooded and kept clear of the deposits that can so easily cause a serious blaze. Have buckets of sand and water placed on strong hooks at strategic points and see that they are always kept fresh and full. Install some of the reputable fire-extinguisher equipment that is nationally advertised. Make rules about smoking by staff. A total ban often encourages surreptitious puffs, with added risk of fire if the offenders imagine that someone in authority is approaching, so it is best to allow it in certain parts of the premises, but not in kitchens, larders, service-rooms and storerooms.

The foregoing applies to nearly all catering establishments. In hotels and the like, some added precautions are essential. Here there is a collection of persons, unknown to each other, living and sleeping in a strange building. It is probable that more people have lost their lives through panic than by actual fire. See that in all corridors, stairways and at other vulnerable points lights are left burning all night. Arrange for every bed to have a light with an easily accessible switch. Emergency exits should be boldly marked so that even an excitable person could not fail to find them—and all doors should open outwards. Should the establishment be large enough to merit a night porter, make absolutely certain not only of his integrity, but also of his reaction in a crisis. Finally, provide plenty of ashtrays and, in all public places, deep receptacles half filled with sand.

POWERS OF LOCAL AUTHORITIES

Investigation should always be made into the various powers of the local authorities in such matters as public safety. When buildings are being constructed or alterations made, plans have to be submitted so that the appropriate authority may examine them, especially relating to entrances, exits, gangways, stairs, passages, etc., and the normal number of persons likely to use the premises. In the case of high buildings there is strict investigation into possible fire risks. Advertisements are frequently restricted in size and position.

In most places collection of refuse from catering establishments is treated as a domestic matter, but if more than the normal number of collections is desired, an extra charge may be made. Kitchen waste is now collected by the local authorities in many areas. Licences to collect such waste may be granted by the Ministry of Agriculture and Fisheries. These, however, are mainly confined to pre-war collectors of swill, who have the requisite plant to deal with this type of waste.

Water for catering establishments is usually supplied through a meter at so much a thousand gallons.

All rateable values are now fixed by the Inland Revenue Department, instead of by local authorities as previously. In the last valuation (1962) hotels and restaurants, which are classified as commercial premises, lost the valuable 20 per cent reduction in rateable value which they had previously enjoyed with shops and offices. It should be noted, however, that appeals against rating assessments can be lodged at any time, although new assessments are normally made only every five years.

INCOME TAX

Most business enterprises are assessed under Schedule D., Case 1. It should be noted that the net profit shown by the profit and loss account is seldom, if ever, the figure upon which tax is levied. There are various adjustments that must be made in order to comply with the income-tax laws. For example, certain expenses charged may not be allowable; credits to profit and loss account may not be taxable. Seldom do sums written off for depreciation agree with the wear-and-tear allowances.

In the main, however, nearly all normal working expenses are allowed. Bad debts (actual) are allowed, but doubtful debts may not be allowed. Legal expenses directly incurred in the business, such as for recovery of debts, would be passed. Legal expenses of a new lease are frequently added to the cost of the lease.

In the catering industry generally, the cost of meals and maintenance of staff, etc. is usually credited to the trading account and debited as a specific charge to the profit and loss account, but proportions applicable to the proprietor must be added back, not being considered allowable. Estimated annual value of accommodation used by the owner and his family must also be added back.

All charges for hire purchase must be allocated between interest, which is allowed, and part hire purchase, which is allocated in reduction of indebtedness—that is, the principal sum. Wear-and-tear allowances can be claimed on furniture, fittings, soft furnishings, etc., except where items subject to constant renewal are so included in the profit and loss account.

The question of employees' income tax is dealt with in Chapter V.

CHAPTER III

The Legal Side—Limited Liability Companies—Partner·
ships—Registration of Business Names—Licensed
Premises—Food and Pests—Various Licences—Some
Legal Terms and Definitions

THE LEGAL SIDE

THE law relating to the catering industry is drawn from
several Acts of Parliament—for example, the Licensing
Acts and the Hotel Proprietors Act, but much of it is that
accumulation of centuries of customs based on decisions
arrived at in courts all over the country. This is known as
common law.

The widespread nature of the activities of the industry
makes for the daily contact of millions of persons: owners,
staff, guests, patrons, suppliers of goods, and very many
others engaged in varied vocations. Whatever number of
disputes may and do arise, comparatively few ever reach
the courts for legal settlement.

The relationship of master and servant, of proprietor
and guest or patron, and certain other questions of law
are dealt with elsewhere in these pages. This chapter is
confined to legal points on which the prospective or new
hotelier or caterer may seek guidance.

LIMITED LIABILITY COMPANIES

In the eyes of the law a limited liability company is
regarded as a separate entity or person from the persons
comprising it. By law it has also a perpetual existence
and succession, and within its common seal can signify
its will in written documents.

The important point about this form of business association is that the liability of the members or shareholders is definitely limited to the amount of shares held. If these are fully paid up, then, whatever may happen, their liability is fully satisfied. Should the shares be partly paid up, then, in the event of a liquidation due to failure of the company, they are liable only for the balance outstanding. Claims for the settlement of debts by all persons, firms, companies and others who have supplied goods or performed services are restricted to the actual property of the company.

A limited company, being a distinct legal personality, can own and deal with property, can sue and be sued, and can execute contracts on its own behalf.

In general, the rights of the shareholders are confined to receiving from the company their share of available profits in the shape of dividends and, on a winding-up, such share of surplus assets as may be available after meeting all liabilities.

There are two classes of limited liability company: public and private. A minimum of seven members is required for the former, a minimum of two for the latter. In each case it is essential to frame what is known as a memorandum of association. This document is really the charter of the company and must contain the following information:—

1. The name of the company with " Limited " as its last word.

2. The situation of the registered office, i.e. in England, which includes Wales, or in Scotland.

3. The objects of the company.

4. A statement that the liability of the members is limited.

5. A statement of the amount of the share capital, and its division into shares of fixed amount and distinct classes.

The memorandum of association must be signed by each subscriber, who must take at least one share. All signatures must be witnessed.

The choice of a name is important, for before attempting to register the company, the proposed name must be submitted to the Board of Trade for approval. The decision of the Board of Trade is final. Later in its life a limited company can, if it so desires, change its name, but again must obtain the approval of the Board of Trade. Note should be made that the name of the company must be displayed outside the registered office, and must also appear on all stationery connected with the business of the company.

The most important clause is, of course, the objects clause. It must state fully and explicitly the objects proposed to be undertaken, as legally no company can undertake any business not so authorized. It is usual to set out the clauses in this section very fully, so as to include everything the company may desire to undertake now and in the foreseeable future, as well as " all such things as may be deemed incidental or conducive to the attainment of the above objects of any of them ".

Under the Companies Act, 1948, a company may alter its objects by passing a special resolution.

Another important document is called the articles of association, which are the rules, so to speak, that govern the internal conduct of the company. They usually cover such matters as the election, retiral and dismissal of directors; shareholders, shares, transfers, etc.; payment of interest; meetings of shareholders; resolutions of various kinds; the secretary; the auditors; winding-up.

During recent years an increasing number of private limited companies have been formed. These associations are invaluable for small and medium-sized family and private businesses desiring the benefit of limited liability. As already mentioned, two persons can form such a company, but intimation must be made on registration that the company restricts the rights to transfer its shares, and limits the number of its members to fifty, exclusive of employees and ex-employees.

Company meetings are of four kinds:—

1. **Statutory.**—This applies to public companies only. It is held not earlier than one month and not more than three months after the date on which the company is entitled to commence business. A full report is made of the preliminary activities of the company in relation to allotment of shares, cash received, directors, secretary and auditors, and particulars of any contract.

2. **Annual General.**—This meeting is held once every calendar year. Not more than fifteen months may elapse between two consecutive meetings.

3. **Extraordinary.**—The directors are usually empowered by the articles of association to convene extraordinary meetings. Period of notice is dependent on the type of resolution to be passed. Should special circumstances arise, shareholders of, say, one-tenth of the paid-up capital of the company may themselves call such a meeting, provided the directors have refused to call it upon previous requisition.

4. **Class.**—These are meetings of shareholders holding a certain class or type of share, and may be called when proposals are made to vary the rights of such shareholders.

Meetings of directors are held as and when required. In many companies it is customary to hold them monthly. Auditors are appointed at each annual general meeting, but, provided they are willing to continue in office or are not disqualified in any way, and that no resolution has been passed by the shareholders appointing some other auditor, the annual re-election is not now necessary.

Various returns must be made at the time of the proposed

B

registering of the company, annually and upon certain changes, etc., taking place, e.g. change of registered address; change in directors; and of any mortgages or similar charges. Professional help in all these matters can be obtained from the accountant and/or auditor to the company, or from the company's solicitors.

PARTNERSHIPS

These are controlled by the Partnership Act, 1890, and the Limited Partnership Act, 1907. Although not absolutely conclusive, the following is the legal definition: " Partnership is the relation which subsists between persons carrying on a business in common with a view to profit."

Generally partners are ordinary or limited. The former takes a full share in the management of the partnership business and, in the event of bankruptcy, is liable, if need be, to the full extent of his assets. A limited partner is liable only up to the sum he has invested in the business, but he cannot take any part in the actual management, except to inspect the partnership books, examine its state of prospects and confer with and advise his co-partners. In addition to the above, there can be a dormant or sleeping partner, who has capital invested, but does not take any active part in the management; and a quasi-partner, who has retired from active participation, but has left his capital as a loan, receiving fixed interest thereon or varied rate of interest according to profits.

Partnerships may be formed by one of three methods: parole agreement, partnership agreement, and partnership deed. The last is preferable in all circumstances, as it sets out clearly all matters relating to capital, interest thereon (if any), division of profit and loss, drawings, drawing up of profit and loss account and balance sheet, fixing good-will on death or retirement of a partner, method of valuation of goodwill, and many other points that may and do arise in the course of the relationship.   The addition of an arbitration clause is commendable.

No partnership may consist of more than twenty partners, and where there are limited partners, there must be general partners also.

REGISTRATION OF BUSINESS NAMES

Subject to the provisions of the Business Names Act, 1916:—

(a) Every firm having a place of business in the United Kingdom and carrying on business under a business name which does not consist of the true surnames of all partners who are individuals and the corporate names of all partners who are corporations without any addition other than the true Christian names of the individual partners or initials of such Christian names;

(b) Every individual having a place of business in the United Kingdom and carrying on business under a business name which does not consist of his true surname without any addition other than his true Christian names or the initials thereof;

(c) Every individual or firm having a place of business in the United Kingdom, who, or a member of which, has either before or after the passing of this Act changed his name except in the case of a woman in consequence of marriage;

(d) Every company as defined in the Companies Act, 1929, carrying on business under a business name which does not consist of its corporate name without any addition

shall be registered in the manner directed by this Act: Provided that:—

(i) where the addition merely indicates that the business is carried on in succession to a former owner of the business, that addition shall not of itself render registration necessary; and

(ii) where two or more individual partners have the same surname, the addition of an *s* at the end of that surname shall not of itself render registration necessary; and

(iii) where the business is carried on by a trustee in bankruptcy or a receiver or manager appointed by any court, registration shall not be necessary; and

(iv) a purchase or acquisition of property by two or more persons as joint tenants in common is not in itself to be deemed carrying on a business whether or not the owners share any profits arising from the sale thereof.

Section 18 of the Act provides that all letter-headings, circulars, etc. must show the present Christian names or initials and surname of each partner and individual, and any former Christian names and surnames, and nationality if this is not British.

Registration must be made with the Registrar of Business Names at London or Edinburgh, the former applying to England, the latter to Scotland. Stamp duty is a 5*s*. adhesive postage stamp.

LICENSED PREMISES

The law relating to the retail sale of intoxicating liquor in England and Wales is laid down in a number of Acts of Parliament, of which the most important are the Licensing Act, 1953, and the Licensing Act, 1961. Scotland has separate laws, which are mainly covered in the Licensing (Scotland) Acts of 1903 and 1959.

Two official documents must be obtained before liquor can be sold to the public: in England a justices' licence and an excise licence; in Scotland a justices' certificate and an excise licence. Applications for justices' licences are considered at special courts held at least five times a year;

in Scotland licensing courts meet half-yearly. Notice of application for a licence must be given in specified form, and usually the assistance of a local solicitor is advisable, both to ensure that all the formalities are properly observed and then to present the application to the court.

The grant of a justices' licence or certificate does not alone authorize the holder to sell liquor; it merely authorizes him to hold an excise licence, and this must be obtained from the Customs and Excise authorities. The excise licence—normally, but not necessarily, granted automatically to the holder of a justices' licence—costs from £5 a year for a full on-licence to £1 10s. a year for a licence to sell only beer or wines.

The justices may refuse to grant a full licence, but if they do so the applicant can appeal to quarter sessions. Interested parties may oppose the grant of a new licence and, if unsuccessful, may also appeal to quarter sessions, asking for the grant to be revoked.

Under the 1961 Act three new types of licence were created which are of special interest to caterers and owners of unlicensed hotels and guest houses. These are: (i) a restaurant licence for the sale of drinks with table meals; (ii) a residential licence for the sale of drink to residents in private hotels, boarding houses, etc.; (iii) a combined residential and restaurant licence for residential establishments with a public restaurant.

Licensing justices may not refuse the grant or renewal of one of these licences except, broadly speaking, on grounds connected with the character of the applicant, the suitability of the premises and the way in which they have been conducted, the extent to which they are patronized by young persons and, in the case of a restaurant licence or combined residential and restaurant licence, on the ground that the trade in table meals is not substantial. The justices can also refuse a licence if the provision of intoxicants would be by " self-service " methods.

Licensing justices can also grant licences subject to a condition that during a part of the year there shall be no permitted hours in the premises, i.e. seasonal licences. The sale of drink with meals may also be allowed on week-days for one hour after the normal closing hour (the supper certificate). Special certificates can also be obtained permitting drinks to be served with meals until 2 a.m. (3 a.m. in London) when music and dancing are provided.

Application can be made for an occasional licence, which is an excise licence granted to enable a person already holding an on-licence to sell liquor on unlicensed premises on the occasion of some function such as a dinner or a dance.

The following are some of the principal points to be observed in the conduct of licensed premises:—

1. The full name of the holder of the licence, together with a note as to whether the licence is " on " or " off " and the liquors that can be sold, must be displayed in a conspicuous place as directed.

2. The Customs and Excise Department must be informed of each building, room, cellar, etc. where liquor is kept.

3. The licence must be produced on demand to an officer of the Customs and Excise Department, a member of the police force, and any justice.

4. Except to hotel residents and their *bona fide* guests, no sale or consumption of liquor may take place on licensed premises outside permitted hours. These hours are fixed by local magistrates in each area.

5. Extensions of permitted hours for special times (Bank Holidays, New Year's Eve, etc.) can be granted by the justices.

6. Young people under eighteen must not be employed in a bar during permitted hours, nor may they be served with intoxicating liquor.

7. Children under fourteen must not be allowed to enter a bar during permitted hours.

8. Police inspection can take place during permitted hours, and also during the period of an extended or occasional licence.

9. Care must be taken that no form of gaming takes place. It is advisable to make full inquiries of the local authorities on this rather complicated subject before allowing or introducing a pastime that might contravene existing bye-laws.

10. Offences committed by licence-holders are fairly heavily punished by law, and sometimes lead to forfeiture of licence.

11. Every retailer of spirits must keep a spirits stock book, in which to record all movements of spirits in and out of the premises. A certificate must accompany each delivery, and no quantity greater than one bulk gallon may be removed without obtaining a certificate from the officer of Customs and Excise.

HYGIENE REGULATIONS

Hygiene regulations which apply to all hotels, restaurants and canteens have been issued under the Food and Drugs Act, 1955. Briefly, the regulations require all catering premises and equipment to be so kept that food is not exposed to contamination. All staff handling food are required to observe cleanly and hygienic methods, including the covering of cuts and abrasions and notification of certain diseases. Smoking is forbidden in rooms where unwrapped food is kept.

Caterers must have adequate supplies of constant hot water, sinks and washing facilities, and must also make arrangements to store safely all foods subject to bacterial infection and multiplication. These foods include meat, poultry, game, fish, gravy, imitation cream, eggs and milk.

Local authorities enforce the regulations, and the order provides for penalties up to £100 fine or three months imprisonment, or both, and fines of up to £5 per day for continuing offences.

Convicted offenders (if the court thinks it expedient in view of the gravity of the offences or the unsatisfactory nature of the premises) may, on the application of the local authority, be disqualified from using the premises for catering for up to two years.

VARIOUS LICENCES

Cinematograph.—Where inflammable films are used in a building for public exhibition of pictures, a licence is required from the Borough Council or City Borough Council. Strict compliance is necessary with all the regulations relating to public safety. Where non-inflammable films are used for exhibiting pictures to hotel guests, no licence is necessary.

Music and Dancing.—Here the law is not uniform throughout the country, and inquiry should be made of the local authority. Generally no licence is required where music and dancing are provided for a private function, i.e. where guests are invited by a host or hostess, and also where tickets are sold to members and friends of associations and similar bodies holding their annual reunions, etc. Licences are, however, required for all public functions where presumably tickets can be purchased by all and sundry, or may even be purchased at the door by anyone passing.

Billiards.—Where premises are fully licensed, no licence is required, but if a room or portion of the premises is used for the playing of billiards *publicly*, a licence is necessary.

Tobacco, etc. Tobacco licences were abolished in the 1963 Budget. Where hotels are fully licensed, tobacco, etc. can be sold during permitted hours, but strictly speaking sale may also be regulated by hours observed by the local shops.

Wireless and Television.—One licence taken out by the owner of a *bona-fide* hotel covers the use on the premises of any number of receiving sets and leads from the main set, whether or not a full excise licence is held, so long as accommodation exists for guests. In a private hotel somewhat similar conditions prevail, except that where separate installations or leads from the main set are installed in *private* rooms, it is necessary to purchase additional licences as required.

Performing Rights.—The Performing Right Society Ltd. deals with this matter by acting on behalf of nearly every owner of copyright music, and issuing the necessary licences to hotels, restaurants, etc. Fees are payable yearly and are usually based on the annual cost of such entertainment. The various means whereby copyright music can be performed are: (*a*) artistes in person, which may comprise individuals, orchestras, dance bands, etc.; (*b*) wireless set, either radio or television; (*c*) gramophone records. In the case of (*c*) care must be exercised, as the High Court has decided that for the record itself a separate copyright exists, so two licences may be required when both music and record are copyright. It can be mentioned that the copyright of practically all records is held by Phonographic Performance Ltd.

Entertainment Duty.—Where entertainment such as music, dancing and cabaret show is provided by a hotel or restaurant without a *separate* charge, or no distinction is made in the charge for the meal, duty is not payable.

The general complexity of the law makes it strongly advisable to seek expert opinion in all cases of doubt. Solution of difficulties and elaboration of regulations can be obtained from the local authority, the trade association or a solicitor. It is decidedly wiser to exercise caution than to rush into a position from which retreat may well prove costly, damaging and rather undignified.

SOME LEGAL TERMS AND DEFINITIONS

A contract is an agreement between two or more persons, which can be legally enforced by law. A simple contract can be created in one of three ways: verbally, by implication, or by writing not under seal.

An agent is a person having authority, either express or implied, to represent or to act on behalf of another person, called the principal. The object is that of bringing the principal into legal relationship with third parties.

A lien (possessory) is the right of an innkeeper, in possession of any luggage belonging to a guest who has failed to pay his bill, to retain such luggage until the bill is settled.

A child is a person under fourteen years of age. A young person is one over fourteen but under eighteen.

Fully licensed premises are those where the sale of practically all wines, spirits, beer, etc. is authorized for consumption both on and off the premises.

Hospitium refers to the area occupied by an inn. It includes all ground attached thereto, particularly the space used as a car park by travellers, guests and others.

CHAPTER IV

**Maintenance of the Building—Maintenance of Installa-
tions—Light, Heat and Ventilation—Wise Selection of
Equipment—Furnishings—Linen—China and Glass—
Cutlery and Silverware—Kitchen and Service-room
Equipment—Keeping an Inventory—Planning the
Kitchen—Refrigeration**

MAINTENANCE OF THE BUILDING

On the acquisition of a hotel, restaurant, tea-room or
whatever it may be, consideration must be constantly given
to its maintenance. If the premises are freehold, full
responsibility rests upon the owner to see that they are
kept in first-class external and internal repair; if they are
leasehold, the liabilities of lessor and lessee will be set out
in the agreement.

Endeavour should always be made to maintain the
premises in the highest possible state of efficiency. In the
long run it is the best and cheapest policy. Should it ever
be decided to sell, then, all things being equal, a full price
can be demanded in the knowledge that the figure is entirely justified.

Give regular attention to the structure. Arrange for
the roofs to be inspected twice a year: once in the early
spring, which will reveal any defects caused by the winter
storms, snow and frost; and again in the late autumn,
which will ensure freedom from dampness and possible
flooding due to accumulation of leaves, dirt and dust in
the gullies, drains, etc. Ascertain that all slates or tiles
are rigid and that the brickwork does not need repointing.
This only requires to be done every seven to ten years, but
local climate may necessitate more frequent applications.

Then there is the matter of the external painting to walls,
etc., if the structure is not built of good stone, although

this, too, is often painted. Paint acts as a splendid pre-
servative, but be careful when deciding on a particular
colour or shade. White is popular, yet it so quickly
becomes greyish, especially in towns. Cream generally
stands up better. Regular outside painting of window-
frames and doors serves the double purpose of preserving
the woodwork and presenting a pleasant appearance to
passers-by.

Attention must be given to all windows, skylights, etc.,
both externally and internally. Make absolutely certain
that they are wind- and water-tight; that the woodwork
and sash-cords are in sound condition. Keep all ventilators
free of dust and dirt, avoiding thereby the loss of valuable
warm air through having to open windows to obtain
fresh air.

Internal decoration is largely a matter of personal
choice. In the case of hotels especially, it is wise to
engage the services of experts. Careful thought given to
various schemes of decoration amply repays. To-day
patrons are very much alive to artistic appearances, and if
the front hall, foyer, lounges and dining-room are tastefully decorated, the premises will make an instant appeal.
The same degree of thought should be given to all bedrooms. Patterned wallpaper is not now fashionable, and
generally a plain paper having tinges of yellow and gold
shades assists in promoting brightness and suggestion of
sunshine. Despite the difficulty of keeping all woodwork
clean and fresh, white and cream are popular, and certainly
present a pleasant appearance. Wherever possible all
toilets and bathrooms should be tiled, or at least painted
or enamelled with the best materials available.

The same attention should be devoted to the working
section of the establishment: kitchen, service-rooms,
larders, still-room, stores and staff quarters. An employer
owes it to his staff and to his business that these quarters
should be kept in first-class condition. How important

this is now considered is evidenced by the passing of the
Food and Drug Act, which requires a much higher degree
of cleanliness in every establishment handling food and
food products.

MAINTENANCE OF INSTALLATIONS

It is recommended that at least twice each year experts
be called in to examine and report on the plumbing, heating
and electrical installations. Damage caused to premises
by faulty plumbing and heating apparatus can prove very
costly, besides dislocating the service and causing dis-
comfort to patrons, who are entitled to an adequate supply
of hot and cold water, and warmth according to the season
of the year. The lagging of pipes to protect them from
frost and to conserve heat from boilers is a matter of great
importance. Again, the supply of hot water to kitchens
and wash-ups is vitally essential, as is the supply of steam
to kitchen equipment. Inspection of boilers and all
component parts must be carried out in order to comply
with insurance requirements.

A fuse can go in any establishment, but material breakdown of service internally is inexcusable. Give attention
to all switches and plugs. See that the fuse-boards are
provided with diagrams setting out the various lights and
rooms controlled by each fuse; and keep a reserve of fuse
wire in each box. Have a supply of correct voltage lamps
conveniently placed on each floor. Remember that the
cost of a lamp may possibly save a heavy claim by someone
for an avoidable accident.

Should the premises be of sufficient size to warrant one
or more permanent maintenance engineers, the money is
well spent. Instant attention can be given to light
failures, lift breakdowns, plumbing defects, and mishaps
to kitchen equipment.

Where metered gas and electric fires are provided in

bedrooms, make certain that each one is efficient and that
the meter is correctly set to supply gas or current of a
quantity at a price to cover adequately your costs and leave
a little over for service in providing the appliances and
clearing the meters from time to time.

LIGHT, HEAT AND VENTILATION

As with decoration, much time, money and effort can be
wasted on these by lack of knowledge and tightness of cash.
In the long run, even if the premises are comparatively
small, it is wise to engage the services of people who know
and who make it their business to give sound advice *and*
service.   A few extra pounds spent at the commencement
will be saved by having a good job of work done, which
will look well and last, rather than a cheap job, which looks
cheap and proves expensive in the end.   Advice on lighting may eventually save pounds in lighting bills, besides
adding to the general efficiency of the business.

For cooking and heating there are five agents from
which to choose: coal, coke, calor gas, gas and electricity.
Each has its strong points, but everything depends upon
the location of the business, its size, the availability of one
or more agents, and the relative costs of installation and
running.   Gas and electricity score over coal and coke in
that there is no labour involved in handling, disposal of
cinders, etc.   They are clean, fume-free and controllable,
and the equipment is easily kept in order.   Nevertheless,
where supplies of solid fuel are near at hand, the price
reasonable, and storage available, it is well worth some
consideration.   Its installation makes for complete in-
dependence of any failure of gas and electricity supplies.
There is on the market some excellent solid-fuel-burning
equipment backed by a fine record of achievement.   Calor
gas is eminently suitable for remote locations.

The highest wisdom is to employ *two* agents for cooking

and heating, so that in the event of a breakdown, shortage of supplies, strikes or inclement weather, the establishment has still a sporting chance of functioning reasonably efficiently.

Ventilation of the premises is extremely important. No patron likes to be either blown out of the premises or to know what is on the menu before he has even had an opportunity to consult it. Guard against condensation and humidity, which latter has an important effect on the heat and cold felt by patrons and staff alike. The installation of thermal equipment effects great saving of fuel. It is advisable, however, to consult an expert before deciding to invest in such apparatus.

WISE SELECTION OF EQUIPMENT

Whatever may be the size of the establishment, the provision of the necessary furnishings, fittings, equipment, china, glass, cutlery, etc., involves considerable outlay. Every item is a valuable asset and essential to the carrying on of the business. Before setting out to purchase all or any of these requirements always invoke the aid of the experts in the particular sphere. Be diligent in the search for just the right article or piece of equipment and at a price you can afford to pay. When choosing equipment keep in mind: (a) location, i.e. buying and delivery facilities; (b) class of patron; (c) type or style of food to be served; (d) hours of service of the main or cooked meals; (e) any structural features that may determine type or size of equipment; (f) length of lease, if the premises are not owned; and (g) facilities for servicing.

In the catering industry every item is subject to really hard usage. It is wisest to purchase from reputable suppliers who regularly advertise in the trade press. As regards kitchen and service-room equipment any of the large manufacturers are ever ready to supply estimates, plan kitchens, etc., and provide every possible after-service to ensure complete satisfaction. It is well worth while to pay visits to other establishments to view similar equipment. Here you will get frank opinions from managers and chefs, and thus effectively verify the claims made by the manufacturers. Of course, sometimes circumstances exist when it is good policy to purchase locally. Patronage begets patronage, and your hotel lounge or tea-room may become a show place of the district, and incidentally a recognized social rendezvous.

If opening an entirely new establishment prepare a detailed budget of costs before commencing to buy. Be perfectly honest with yourself. You know just how much you can afford to spend. Besides keeping within that sum, see that your suggested expenditure is properly apportioned to the various classes of furnishing and equipment.

As the larger items of kitchen equipment are fairly costly give consideration to the actual and near-future requirements of your business. Exercise care that you purchase the right type and number, and have no surplus or misfits. Before finally deciding make quite certain that all facilities for the supply of gas and/or electricity are readily available, and that adequate drainage is accessible.

In the post-war years great strides have been made in the production of all kinds of furnishing and equipment. Many of these save labour, give increased service and promote higher production all round. With adequate care and constant servicing, carpets will last from five to seven years; cutlery and silverware from twenty to twenty-five years; kitchen equipment from fifteen to twenty years. Wise outlay and careful selection will be amply repaid in the years to come.

FURNISHINGS

For public rooms such as the lounge and dining-room it is, of course, essential for the furnishings to blend with the proposed scheme of decoration. Each room should be decorated and furnished as a complete unit. Nothing should clash. Avoid the bizarre and keep to pastel shades, which promote restfulness for mind and body.

Make certain that every chair is designed to provide the maximum comfort. In the main lounge, chairs are usually comfortable, but in many dining-rooms they leave much to be desired. Ensure that all chairs can be easily cleaned and are sufficiently well built to stand up to hard usage. Seats that can be lifted out are recommended. Where patrons include a fair number of children, a few suitable chairs for them, especially in the dining-room, are much appreciated by parents and guardians.

Tables should be of various sizes, seating two, four, six and eight persons. Round tables are popular, especially with small parties. Oblong tables, with two pull-out ends, are suitable for ten to twelve persons, and invaluable at functions calling for a top table and " sprigs ". It is still undecided whether the provision of an under-shelf for ladies' handbags and parcels is essential. Though definitely convenient, they do so often provide items for the lost-property section.

Glass-topped tables are now somewhat out of fashion, for there are so many new substitutes on the market. Completely resistant in the main to all spills of liquor, cigarette burns, etc., and easily cleaned with a damp cloth, they are eminently suitable for lounges, bars, snack-bars and the like.

Dining-room tables should be covered with white or cream baize. This in time gets rather soiled and cleaning becomes a problem. One solution is to make use of old tablecloths as under-cloths, as they can be easily laundered.

Unless there is a gentlemen's cloakroom it is necessary to provide hat-and-coat stands. They should be strong and securely fastened to floor, wall or pillar, to prevent accidents through the collapse of a heavily laden and un-balanced stand.

Dumb-waiters should be of sufficient size to allow of two waiters or waitresses making full use of them. The top should be covered with some heat-resisting material. Above it should be another two shelves, the upper one slightly less deep than the lower; below it should be pigeon-holes for cutlery, these covered with green baize, while the lower shelf or shelves can be used for cruets, glasses, roll-baskets, etc.

The floors of the public rooms should be of good hard wood, easily polished and providing an excellent surface for dancing. Floor coverings are usually of carpet, especially in lounges, dining-rooms and bedrooms. These are either fitted or squares. In the long run it will be found that squares are best, as they can be turned in order to wear evenly. Should the dining-room or lounge be large, have several squares of carpet. They can be securely fixed by long brass nails passed through rings in the carpet and then into sockets in the wooden floor.

When choosing carpets employ experts. Remember that all carpets will be subject to hard wear. They should be of a long-lasting but easily cleaned pile. Colour and design are a matter of blending with the general scheme. Self-coloured are not too profitable; a patterned design of a simple character is recommended.

Where traffic is heavy in foyers, halls, lounges and corridors, there are many excellent rubber combinations. Hard-wearing, safe and pleasant to walk upon, and pleasing to the eye, they can be obtained in a variety of colours and designs. Special preparations are available for efficient cleaning.

It is a matter of taste whether the corridors of the bed-room flats should be similarly covered or whether they should be carpeted. The rubber type of covering is to be preferred. If carpet is decided upon, the side border may be either stained or regularly polished. Stair covering should match the corridor covering.

The furnishing of bedrooms consists of: either a single or double bed, often of the divan type; wardrobe, tallboy and dressing-table; one or two small chairs and at least one occasional or arm-chair; bedside stand and light(s); waste-paper basket; luggage rack or stand. Endeavour should be made to ensure that all furniture blends and that the whole effect is pleasing to the eye. Carpets should preferably be in squares, with the borders stained or polished. Here again, a design is recommended; self-coloured carpets show up every piece of fluff, etc.

Curtains are quite an expensive item, especially in the public rooms, for which they require to be of fairly heavy material, fully lined and of an ample width to give a good appearance. In the bedrooms a lighter material suffices, and here can be introduced curtains of a brighter and patterned type. For toilets and bathrooms plastic curtains are suggested.

The covering of settees in the public rooms is again a matter of blending with the general scheme. Moquette is popular, but there is much to be said in favour of loose covers of chintz, cretonne or one of the many new materials now available. Their merit lies in that they can be washed many times, thus renewing their appearance. All cushions and pillows should have loose covers.

A few standard lamps in the lounge add a very restful touch to the general scene, and a draught screen can be most useful.

It is well-nigh impossible to enumerate all the various fixtures and fittings necessary in a catering establishment. The guiding principle, however, is to exercise care when making every purchase, to ensure that the article is suitable to the particular type of enterprise. The best gives efficient service, has long life and looks good.

LINEN

In view of the hard wear to which linen is subjected, buy the highest quality that you can afford. When setting out to purchase obtain as many prices and samples as possible, so that your choice is wide. Length of service is vital, and a contributory factor is the laundry, the choice of which is just as important as the selection of the linen. It is often wise to pay a slightly higher rate to ensure careful handling and first-class work.

When deciding on a design, choose one that is more or less a stock pattern, so that future matchings will be easy. Much depends upon the class of business, the rate of turn-over and, on the question of quantity, whether functions are to be undertaken. As a guide, however, have in stock three changes of table-cloths and four times your seating capacity in table-napkins. The quantities of cloths for dishes, glass, service and waiters will be determined by the size of the business, but remember that an ample stock is money well spent, for constant use, plus laundry hand-ling, tends to shorten the life of linen, which benefits from a rest. Towels of various sizes for guests should be of good serviceable quality. White is the usual colour, but there are now available many lovely colours and shades, and if you consider that your class of guest would appre-ciate these, then purchase a supply.

Bed linen should also be of the best quality. The quantity required will be determined by the number of beds and whether they are single or double. In these modern times single divans are popular. Blankets, sheets and pillow-cases are the main requirements. Bed-covers and down quilts come under the head of soft furnishings and must tone in with the colour scheme of each bed-room.

Every single article should be permanently and clearly

marked with the initials or name of the proprietor or by some designation pertaining to the establishment. Owing to the high costs prevailing at the present time, strict checking of all linen sent to and returned from the laundry is imperative. Any shortages must be advised at once.

CHINA AND GLASS

The main considerations are: durability, but not too heavy to offend patrons; initial and replacement costs; design pleasing, but easy to keep scrupulously clean. Quantity required will depend upon seating capacity and rate of turnover. Aim at a stock of three times your seating capacity for all items except cups, which, being the heaviest replacement item, should be six times the seating capacity. You will require the following: tea-cups, saucers and plates; coffee-cups and saucers; soup-, fish-, meat-, entrée- and sweet-plates. It is advisable to have your monogram stamped on each piece.

In the case of glassware toughness in service combined with appearance is essential. Should your premises be licensed, a range of glasses for sherry, cocktails, various wines, beer, etc., will be required.

Never use any item of china or glass that is cracked, chipped or discoloured in any way.

CUTLERY AND SILVERWARE

These are fairly expensive and it is advisable to obtain samples and prices from several suppliers. Always purchase from one of the long-established and really reputable firms who constantly advertise in the trade press. Important points are: (*a*) good appearance; (*b*) long service; (*c*) easily washed and cleaned, with no elaborate chasing; (*d*) all tea- and coffee-pots and hot-water jugs to be of such type that the interiors and spouts can be readily cleaned; and (e) facilities available for repairing and renovating.

Cleaning of cutlery, etc., may be by hand or by a burnisher.

KITCHEN AND SERVICE-ROOM EQUIPMENT

Two essential considerations when purchasing equipment are: (a) that the various services—gas, electricity and solid fuel—are adequate; and (b) that the premises have facilities for either or preferably both of the first-mentioned laid on. Before deciding which agent to use, obtain estimates and plans, then visit other premises of a similar type where such plant is in operation and get the opinion of the users. The amount of money required for kitchen and service-room equipment is fairly large, and much thought and care must be given before a final choice is made. Primal installation or change-over later can be extremely costly.

There is now available for kitchens and service-rooms high-class equipment of excellent performance, pleasing design and finish, as well as being easily kept clean. Endeavour to buy only what you actually require for your special purpose, and sufficient to meet all expected demands, leaving a margin for emergencies. The purchase of smaller items such as saucepans, frying pans, strainers, knives and the dozens of other articles essential to production should be entrusted to the chef. Ask him to submit a list of his requirements and prices. By thus placing the responsibility on him, you make him bear the blame should his choice prove unsatisfactory.

Actual requirements can be fairly accurately based on the type of establishment, the accommodation available for such equipment, and, to some extent, the power unit—gas, steam, solid fuel or electricity, or a combination of any of these agents.

Much saving can be effected in the consumption of all fuel by ensuring that the equipment is kept in first-class working order and that the staff is trained to watch constantly for defects and immediately report them.

Items of heavy and light equipment for the kitchen are listed below:—

Heavy	Bain-marie [1]
	Boiling table
	Boiling pan
	Bread- and bacon-slicing machines
	Butter-pat machine
	Cake-mixer, with mincer and accessories
	Central range
	Dish-washing machine
	Fish-fryer
	Griller
	Potato-peeling machine
	Potato chipper
	Potato masher
	Pastry oven
	Steamer
	Stock-pots
	Runs of benching and/or stout tables with drawers
	Tables for crockery, cutlery, etc.
Light	Brushes and brooms
	Bowls, steel, enamel and plastic
	Boards, carving
	Carving knives (various)
	Canisters
	Clock (electric)
	Colanders
	Pastry cutters

[1] For description see page 147.

Can-openers
Ice-cream servers
Stewpans (various sizes)
Frying pans
Pudding bowls
Jugs, enamelled
Scales, automatic and balance
Sieves
Cleaning utensils

KEEPING AN INVENTORY

As you will have invested quite a large proportion of
your capital in equipment, utensils, china, glass, cutlery
and other fittings and fixtures, whether by direct purchase
from suppliers if you have just commenced a new venture,
or by taking over from the former owner, it is imperative
that you prepare and keep up to date a detailed inventory
in an indexed notebook.   Allocate a page to each item and
set out the following details: full description, date of
purchase, name and address of supplier, initial cost, cost
of any major repairs or replacements and dates, depreciation written off each year, and the sum finally obtained on
its sale when worn out or replaced by a more modern
style.   File all bills separately in a folder for easy reference.

This register is invaluable for inventory purposes.
Providing a history of each item, it is extremely useful
when considering replacements, and assists the accountant
when claiming for wear and tear.   By adding up the various
sums expended, the owner will know exactly how much he
has invested.

Large items of equipment, furniture, fittings and cutlery
will not require replacement for some time, but it is wise,
wherever possible, to build up a reserve or replacement
fund from profits, to meet the cost when it does arise.
With china, glass and the smaller utensils the rate of

wastage is higher, and replacements have to be made regularly. By keeping careful records of all such purchases, and by taking regular inventories, a firm check can be kept on all these items.

A weekly inventory is advised. It can easily be taken each Monday morning by the owner and the cashier. In addition to a check of the quantities, it affords an opportunity to examine the condition as to general cleanliness and serviceability. Intensive search should be made for all missing cutlery, etc., as often damaged items are concealed—" planked ", as they call it in the industry—and if not located quickly and repaired, can so easily become rusty and past mending.

Breakages are unavoidable, but by these regular checks and keeping a careful note of all " shorts ", prompt investigation can be made whenever wastage appears excessive. Carelessness may account for a proportion, but so often a reorganization of the method of serving and/or washing-up routine effects much saving.

The time spent on these inventories will show a return, tending to reduce considerably that enemy of catering—waste.

These notes should be read in conjunction with those on costing and control, which form the subject of Chapter VII.

PLANNING THE KITCHEN

Much thought must be given to the kitchen, which, with its ancillary departments, the larder, vegetable-store, preparation-room, pastry-room and service-rooms, is the production centre of your business. Unfortunately many kitchens are situated in the basement, consequently suffering from lack of direct communication with the service section, except by means of lifts and speaking-tubes.

Wherever possible locate the kitchen where it will have natural light, thus saving cost and time, as well as promoting good service to all departments. Devote as much space as possible, with high ceilings, walls of durable, light-reflecting, easily cleaned material, floors of sufficient strength to carry heavy equipment, easily cleaned, non-slippery, resilient to the feet and non-absorbent. Lighting should be generous—in large kitchens, at least one light over each piece of equipment, so placed that the light falls on the plant and not on the user. Avoid glare by fitting translucent bowls. Adequate ventilation is imperative; no kitchen odours should ever penetrate any other portion of the building.

Should there be an opportunity to design a new or modernized kitchen, it is an excellent plan to prepare on paper the area available to scale, and have small pieces of coloured paper cut to scale, each representing a piece of equipment. Spend some time in arranging and rearranging these in an endeavour to arrive at the best possible lay-out. Keep in mind that the preparation and processing of food should flow evenly. As in a motor-car factory, where, by the conveyor-belt system, raw material enters at one end and eventually the completed vehicle is run off at the other end for probable immediate delivery, so a like system ought in very large measure to be in operation in your kitchen. Avoid all bottle-necks. They reduce efficiency, cost time, money and temper.

It is admitted that many small places do not permit of really scientific arrangement, yet much can be done by the small owner who gives this matter mature thought.

Try to place your stove, with its ovens, etc., in the centre of the kitchen, thus giving room for the staff to move around in some degree of comfort. Should there be the risk of fumes, install a ventilation hood and shafting to carry the fumes to the nearest window, where they can be expelled by an electric fan. Have the wash-up and vegetable sinks placed, with adequate draining-boards, round the walls, dealing similarly with the stock-pots and steamer. In fact, try to place every piece of equipment where it will give maximum service. Your staff are paid to work, not walk. If space permits place the work table(s) as centrally as possible, facilitating full use of available space. Plan your serving space so that the waiting staff can speedily deposit used plates, etc., then collect orders from the hot-plate. Next to good cooking and presentation, speed of service is appreciated by patrons. As in war, " too little and too late " spells disaster. Equally, the preparation of excess quantities of food, faulty cooking and preventable waste all lead to a similar tragic end.

The chef should be fully responsible for the whole of this department, including all service-rooms, so that the final stages—the portioning and presentation of the food— are efficiently carried out as a fitting climax to the care, thought and work expended on the food from its raw state.

All service-rooms should be equipped with the necessary hot-plates, etc., to ensure that both food and plates are piping hot when placed before the patron.

REFRIGERATION

Its function is threefold: (a) the storage of meat, fish, fats, etc., in bulk; (b) the storage of prepared vegetables, fruit, ice-cream, etc., to maintain their condition until required for service; and (c) the storage of left-overs.

Due to the activities and multiplication of harmful organisms in the air, food, whether raw or cooked deteriorates rapidly unless placed in efficient cold storage. These bacteria increase rapidly at fifty degrees and over, but at forty-five degrees and below, this activity is checked. Generally all perishables required by caterers should be stored in refrigerators at a temperature of forty degrees.

Refrigerators should never be placed in kitchens, as the heated air and moisture produced by cooking tend to affect their efficient working. The larder or storage-room is ideal.

The arrangement of food in the refrigerator is important. Foods susceptible to tainting from those possessing strong odours should be kept covered and placed in the coldest position—that is, closest to the air stream as it circulates away from the evaporator. Food that smells more strongly should be placed (covered) at the end of the air stream, when deodorization of the air will occur *after* passing over it.

To meet all requirements, refrigerators are operated by gas, electricity or paraffin. Size ranges are manufactured to suit most individual needs and space available. The average weight of foodstuffs stored is three pounds per cubic foot.

New types of catering equipment are constantly coming on to the market and there are particularly noteworthy developments in deep-freeze storage cabinets and microwave ovens. These two items, used together, can supply the entire kitchen equipment to service a busy restaurant. An appropriate supply of pre-cooked, quick-frozen foods are kept in the cabinet, heated as required in a few seconds in the microwave oven, and served.

CHAPTER V

The Human Element—Framing a Labour Policy—
Selection of Staff—Engagement and Payment of Staff—
P.A.Y.E.—National Insurance Act, 1946—Accidents to
Staff—Treatment and Training of New Staff—Staff
Uniforms—Salesmanship—Waiters and Their Duties

THE HUMAN ELEMENT

DURING the past twenty years much greater attention has
been deservedly paid to staff of all grades in every industry
and business organization. Employers in the main now
realize just how vitally important to the success of any
enterprise is the human element, and this is particularly
so in the catering industry, where service is or should be the
watchword, the goal of each establishment, whether it be a
humble snack-bar or a great luxury hotel.

New concepts of the place occupied by management are
now arising and, with few exceptions, the one-time aloof,
far-distant, omnipotent and unapproachable being has
given place to a person who, though still endowed with
authority, is now easily accessible and is usually possessed
of a measure of sweet reasonableness. Primarily the aim
of management should be to create and foster a spirit
among all staff that they are not merely working *for* their
employer, but *with* him. Care, however, must of necessity
be taken that all management is, in the highest sense, *with*
the workers, but not *of* them.

Management in general has been described as an art.
To-day some wish to call it a science, but this seems too
exact, leaving no room for the creative spirit of the individual. The important function of controlling and
directing the labour of human beings requires latitude.

The catering industry is a combination of production

and service, which must be fully co-ordinated to attain a high degree of efficiency. While amicable relations in a factory are of no small importance, in the catering industry they are vital. The demands of the customer are much more immediate, and, unlike the factory product, which can be sold later, food is of such a perishable nature that business lost is gone for ever.

Try to provide a high standard of working conditions and so place yourself in the position to demand a high standard of service from your employees, especially that extra effort required when pressure of business is heavy.

FRAMING A LABOUR POLICY

Whatever may be the size of your business, endeavour to frame a labour policy and, having framed it, see that every employee, from the highest to the lowest, knows exactly how it affects him or her. In large concerns this policy must be fully backed and implemented by top management; so often the laudable intentions of top management are thwarted by the action or inaction of those of supervisory status.

The chief aim of a labour policy is to provide the highest possible level of wages and conditions, consistent with the just claims of the owners, whether private or shareholders, and the patrons. Management must fix wages and salaries that are fair and reasonable, taking into account local conditions and the status of the various employees. It is not imperative that the rates laid down in the Catering Wages Acts be adhered to in their entirety; higher rates are frequently paid and are fully justified.

The creation of an atmosphere in which everyone is happy and willingly gives unstinted service is the ultimate goal. We are all, more or less, sensitive to atmospheres, and so often one comes across establishments where the atmosphere is charged with distrust, apprehension and the sense of insecurity. Consequently the resultant quality of service is low.

From the worker's standpoint two fundamentals emerge: (a) desire for a measure of economic satisfaction with the present condition and future prospects; and (b) a degree of interest and happiness in the particular job which, by its performance, makes it an acceptable way of life.

Evidence that employers do have a real concern for their staff goes a long way in achieving successful management of personnel. All efforts made to inform each worker that his job, however humble it may appear to him, counts in the general scheme are of value. Treatment of all staff as active co-partners in the enterprise, and not as mere cogs in the wheel, and the dissemination of knowledge that all top management is not only fully authorized, but also completely competent, are of immense help towards the attainment of the aim of the owner to give full service to his patrons.

The elaborate welfare schemes of most large organizations undoubtedly achieve much good, but many a smaller establishment, with little or no pretensions to personnel management as such, may have unconsciously secured the same excellent labour relations. Brief, informal chats with employees, either singly or in groups, can work wonders. Encourage them to ask questions and offer suggestions. Give figures showing the cost of replacing china and glass, and the amounts paid out for gas, electricity and power, thereby encouraging economy. Give hints on savings on cleaning materials and on laundry. Show how business may have been lost, but read them letters of appreciation from satisfied patrons.

Physical conditions have a direct bearing on morale. Attention paid to lighting, heating, ventilation, seating arrangements, lavatories, rest-rooms and dining-rooms all makes for loyal service. Group welfare to-day takes many forms, dependent upon the size of the business and the outlook of the chief executives. Opinion is divided: while many firms go all out for such types of welfare as the provision of playing-fields, the encouragement of dramatic societies, debating and literary societies, adult education, etc., other firms look upon all this as an intrusion on the private lives of adult employees. Much, however, can be done in a smaller way by, for example, the provision of suitable rest-rooms, especially in hotels, where, as an alternative to going out in all weathers, the only escape for staff off duty is an unheated, austere bedroom. Provide a few card-tables, a dart-board, perhaps even table tennis. A hand-operated sewing-machine will also be much appreciated by your female staff.

Probably the greatest source of staff troubles is poorness of meals, which are so often of low quality, badly cooked and indifferently served in depressing surroundings. All this leads to petty pilfering and waste of kitchen time and your money in purchasing food that may reach the swill bin. See that your staff are well fed, have proper breaks for meals and, as far as circumstances permit, the time-off periods to which they are entitled. In the case of hotels, where members of the staff live on the premises, make a point of having all staff bedrooms scrupulously clean and suitably furnished according to status.

Provide tip-up seats for female staff who serve or wait upon patrons.

In all establishments there should be a set of rules governing the behaviour of employees in such matters as punctuality, holidays, dress, notification of absence due to illness or domestic troubles, breakages, carrying out of parcels, etc. Endeavour to impose all these rules with firmness and justice. Breaches of timekeeping, and absence through any cause, should be thoroughly investigated before judgment is given.

Strictly forbid smoking except in certain permitted

parts of the premises. Prohibit female staff from applying make-up in public; this should be confined to the
cloakrooms.

It is suggested that, to ensure that all essential duties are
covered each day, a work chart be drawn up, setting out
clearly all daily duties and who is responsible for their
performance.

A good deal depends upon the executive or supervisory
staff, who should endeavour to build up teamwork.
Groups often work unofficially under a leader, which
serves to create and stimulate co-operation, to provide
sociability at meals, and to give an opportunity for forming friendships. Tactful supervisory approach to group
leaders often tends to settle petty differences, and frequently major ones as well.

It is by no means easy to gather together supervisors of
different ages, training, temperament and outlook, and
weld them into one body charged with enthusiastically and
efficiently carrying out to the letter the directions and
intentions of top-level authority.

If the industry is to provide leaders and high executives
for the efficient conduct of its business in the years to
come, a promotion policy must be framed. It must be
fully explained to all concerned and, as an earnest of good
intentions, every facility must be given for suitable
employees to acquire both extensive and intensive training,
under the guidance of efficient and sympathetic supervisors. They must also be encouraged to join classes at
technical colleges, to attend conferences and to visit other
large establishments. In all cases advancement should
only be made in the interests of the business as a whole and
on no other grounds.

While, in the small establishment, the general management and direct supervision rests primarily on the owner,
it is advisable to delegate responsibility for duties. This
is useful in times of sickness, holidays, etc. It also makes

C

those concerned feel that they too have a real stake in the fortunes of the enterprise.

Staff respect executives only when these are fully capable in their jobs, display confidence, and are able to make rapid decisions and originate prompt action. It is unwise for supervisory staff to start shouting and give displays of temper when things go wrong. Sarcasm is not constructive; it leads to resentment and is mortifying to the person at whom it is directed. Know how and when to criticize and praise. Never do it in the presence of other employees. Such reprimands humiliate, such commendation savours of favouritism. When mistakes have been made, get the employee to tell you exactly how it happened. If his story is weak both you and he will soon realize it, and you can possibly look for an early improvement.

Encourage suggestions from your staff; after all, they are in the closest touch with every single operation and with all your patrons. Details that may be of some moment to them may so easily escape your attention. Even if you are unable to act on the suggestion, give it sympathetic consideration and thus leave the door open for the matter to be brought up at a later date.

A word to recently appointed supervisors. Get to know your staff and give them the opportunity to know you. Make notes of all changes you consider advisable, then put them aside for six weeks. Then take them out and read them over, and you will be surprised to find the revision that is required. It is far better to go slowly than to make drastic changes, later followed by reversals.

SELECTION OF STAFF

Too often employers fail to give this aspect of management the attention it deserves. Staff are carelessly chosen and, particularly the rank and file, accept employment in the same haphazard fashion, with the result that, although some are fortunate in finding work that suits them and they can do efficiently and under congenial conditions, many others, unfitted by temperament or lack of training, either leave or are dismissed, thus causing a high labour turnover.

Employers in the industry should realize just how much it costs to interview, engage and possibly train a new entrant, who may quickly prove unsuitable and necessitate a repetition of the whole procedure.

The National Institute of Industrial Psychology has created a seven-point plan that provides a series of categories applicable to the requirements of the job and the qualities of the individual.

1. **Physique.**—Covers health and strength, outward appearance and manner, and physical energy.

2. **Attainments.**—Includes general education, specialized training and actual working experience.

3. **General Intelligence.**—Assessing capacity for clear thinking and arriving at decisions quickly.

4. **Special Attributes.**—Having what may be termed a gift for quickly assimilating a certain type of skill.

5. **Interests.**—That is, apart from occupation or vocation. These may be described as social, intellectual, physically active, and practical constructive.

6. **Disposition.**—The ability or faculty of undertaking responsibility for others' work, action, etc. It also involves level-headedness and general acceptance.

7. **Circumstances.**—Taking into account background circumstances when considering wages, etc.

The principal sources of labour are:—

1. **Applications Received in Response to Advertisements inserted in the Local or National Press.** This usually proves satisfactory, though it must be borne

in mind that many excellent men and women in the industry are not good at expressing themselves to the best advantage on paper, so that until they have been interviewed it is difficult to arrive at a fair decision.

2. **Labour Exchanges.**—These are now really helpful and do try, especially in large cities and resorts, to render efficient service to prospective employers by carefully grading each potential employee. In London there is a Labour Exchange devoted entirely to the catering industry. " Denmark Street ", as it is familiarly called, does excellent work. The address is : 1 Denmark Street, London, W.C.2. (Telephone: Temple Bar 6622.)

3. **Agencies.**—These are in many cases old-established and reliable, and are often patronized by the executive class who may not relish going to a Labour Exchange.

4. **Introductions from Present Employees, Patrons or Business Friends.**—This source frequently presents problems, as such introductions, so often well meant, may lead to friction in the event of the applicant proving unsuitable or unsatisfactory.

5. **Direct Applications.**—These generally should be carefully considered, as at least they show initiative and a desire to succeed.

6. **Training Schools and Colleges.**—A comparatively new and growing source, these are productive of usually keen, intelligent young men and women, most of whom will have completed courses of from two to three years.

Most employers will make use of all these sources during their business careers, but whatever the method it is essential that for *all* jobs an interview be given before a decision is reached.

Interviewing is primarily a matter of matching prospective candidates with vacant posts. To do this efficiently it is advisable to prepare a comprehensive list of all the positions in your business. The schedule should show:—

1. Short description of the work to be performed.
2. Necessary qualifications and experience required.
3. Whether any physical attributes are essential.
4. Whether the work is done singly or as a member of a team.
5. Disposition necessary.
6. Normal working hours per week and the wage or salary.
7. Holidays and any other perquisites.
8. Future prospects (if any).

Each applicant should be required to fill in a simple form giving: (a) full name and address; (b) age; (c) married or single; (d) family (if any); and (e) brief particulars of posts held, commencing with present post or last one held.

Provided with this information an employer can approach with some confidence the task of interviewing. He owes it to himself and to all the candidates that the matter be conducted in a businesslike manner. When arranging interviews he should state the exact location, date and time, and by whom the candidate will be interviewed. Punctuality is important; the candidates may have had to ask for time off, or may even be losing wages. No third party should be present at the interview unless closely affected by the eventual choice.

Conduct the interview fairly quickly. Aim at getting all the information required. Stick to facts. Be natural and endeavour to bring out the best in each candidate. Note the impression made on you by every one of them, and try to be fair when deciding. A relatively poor letter may come from an excellent chef; a well-written letter from a too clever hall-porter. If at all possible notify the result, even by a postcard, to the unsuccessful applicants. Better bad news than suspense.

Opinions vary on the merits of written references. Few of us have read a really bad one! Whenever possible, contact by telephone should be made with a former employer. Many hesitate to express on paper their true feelings on this sometimes delicate matter, but often a friendly chat over the telephone proves of great value to the prospective new employer.

To assist further in the vital matter of staff selection, a few notes are given below:—

Management and Executive.—Should possess wide knowledge and experience of the duties involved, be of good appearance, be tactful, and have a pleasing personality.

Supervisors.—Whilst the authority of supervisors over staff is extensive, that over patrons is limited. The old adage that the customer is always right now demands some modification, and where situations arise when decisions have to be made between patrons and staff, experience and tact are essential in a supervisor. Again, any supervisor who can ease tension caused by temporary shortage of supplies, delays of various kinds, and any dislocation caused by a sudden rise in tempo of business, is worth every penny of his salary.

Office and Control Staff.—Should possess requisite ability to perform all the duties pertaining to this department, and be able to secure the fullest co-operation and respect from all staff.

Cashiers, Reception and Bill Office Staff.—Apart from the required efficiency in their duties, should possess charm of manner, tact, and be able to behave correctly towards patrons. Generally they are the first and last contacts. See that the impression is good.

Waiters and Waitresses.—Requisite skill at their jobs, pleasing personality, good memory, and a calm demeanour. In addition a standard of politeness that neither savours of formal etiquette nor borders on familiarity. Information concerning waiters and their duties appears at the end of this chapter.

Wine Butler.—Must have full knowledge of every wine on the list and be able to advise patrons as to choice. Should know how to make up cocktails and be acquainted with every detail of bar work. In French he is the *sommelier*.

Barmen and Barwomen.—Should have competence in the handling and serving of all liquors, and should above all be honest. In view of the high value of the stock involved, all temptation or opportunity to "fiddle" should be reduced as far as humanly possible by the control system (see Chapter VIII).

American Barmen.—Must have expert knowledge of all the most popular cocktails, of which there are to-day many hundreds.

Chef and Kitchen Staff.—As chief of production the chef is the cornerstone of the business. Apart from culinary skill he should possess the virtue of being a disciplinarian, a teacher and a leader. In fairness he should be party in the engagement of all kitchen and service-room staff, which has the added advantage of giving him a share in the responsibility when things go wrong. The size of the business determines the number of the kitchen staff. There may be need for assistant chefs, cooks dealing with various kinds of cooking such as pastry and sweet production, together with such clerical assistance as may be necessitated by the daily recording of all movements of food, by the control system and by periodical stocktakings.

Housekeeper.—Should be a paragon of all the virtues: competence in all housewifely duties, ability to control all staff, common sense, clear judgment, ready sympathy, quick understanding, and a well-developed sense of humour.

Telephonists.—Should have the necessary technical skill, clear, mellow voices, perfect diction, and a pleasing, helpful manner.

Front-of-the-House Staff.—Should be of good appearance, intelligent, and possessed of a pleasing and helpful manner. They should have full knowledge of local transport and events, as well as being able to give clear directions to all motorists.

Engineers and Maintenance Staff.—Should be well qualified in their respective trades and have a high standard of integrity. They should be able to meet every emergency in their particular spheres.

Night Porters and Watchmen.—Fullest investigation should be made as to character and general background. They may be called upon to act promptly and efficiently in the event of such happenings as fire during the night.

ENGAGEMENT AND PAYMENT OF STAFF

The basic factors in the relations between employer and staff are embodied in common law. In addition, many hotel and catering workers are covered by statutory regulations issued under the Catering Wages Act (now replaced by the Wages Councils Act). These regulations cover all staff working in licensed hotels, inns, restaurants and canteens, but not unlicensed hotels, boarding houses, hospitals or schools. They specify minimum wage rates for all grades of staff and also cover holiday pay and certain conditions of work. Copies of the relative orders are available at H.M. Stationery Office and are sent out to employers affected by the Office of Wages Councils, Ebury Bridge House, Ebury Bridge Road, London, S.W.1.

The Shop Acts, which apply to certain workers, set out various rules dealing with meal- and rest-breaks and time off. The Truck Acts, which now apply to all manual workers and craftsmen, ensure that all wages are paid in cash, prohibiting employers from paying in kind or making deductions of a similar nature.   Legal deductions from wages are mainly for national insurance and income tax (P.A.Y.E.).

It is wise to familiarize oneself with all the regulations and, by careful attention to them, earn from one's employees efficient and loyal service based on mutual respect and the guarantee of always getting a square deal.   Apart from this, it is a certainty that one day some smart employee will demand some possibly obscure right laid down in some sub-section of a section of one of these Acts.

Under the new Contract of Employment Bill, now going through Parliament and expected to become law in the spring of 1964, every permanent employee will have to be given a written contract and a minimum period of notice.

The Bill provides that an employee who has been continuously employed for between two and five years will be entitled to a minimum period of notice of two weeks.   An employee who has been employed continuously for a period of more than five years will be entitled to a minimum of four weeks notice.   During the period of notice the employee will be entitled to pay at a rate not less than his average rate of pay in the previous six months.

The Bill also provides that each employee who normally works at least twenty-one hours weekly must be given, within five weeks of starting, a written statement specifying his terms of employment.   This must cover: (a) rate of pay, and method of calculation; (b) whether payment is to be made weekly, monthly or at other intervals; (c) any terms or conditions relating to hours of work; (d) any terms and conditions relating to holidays and holiday pay, sick pay and pensions; and (e) length of notice (covering the first two years).

This new legislation will undoubtedly have a far-reaching effect in the hotel and catering industry and will sound the death knell of the old system under which staff could be dismissed or could walk out at a moment's notice. It will not be possible for an employer to contract out of the main provisions of the Bill, except to give staff rights which are equal to, or better than, those laid down.

Make sure that when occasion arises to give summary dismissal you are on perfectly safe legal ground. Due care must also be taken when proposing to make deductions from wages in respect of fines, errors made in bills, shortages of cash, breakages, etc. In the case of the first two, full evidence, i.e. kitchen and cash checks relating to the error, should always be produced. Deductions for breakages and damage to fittings, plant, equipment and utensils are very frequently fraught with danger, as much depends upon the circumstances. Of course, if the breakage and/or damage be deliberate, dismissal is the only answer.

Upon engagement and commencing duty the new entrant should hand in his P.A.Y.E. Form (P45) and national insurance card. For foreigners arriving in this country to work, it is necessary to obtain permits, some of which require renewal from time to time. The local Labour Exchange will supply information on this matter.

Whilst it is not compulsory, all employers are expected to employ disabled persons on the basis of three per cent, provided that the total number of employees exceeds twenty. These disabled persons are those who are permanently incapacitated, by reason of injury, disease, deformity, or by disablement due to war injuries, industrial and road accidents, from obtaining employment and earning reasonable wages.

Permanent records are extremely important in these days of close association with Government departments. Whatever may be the size of your establishment, aim at keeping a record of all employees, past and present. The simpler the system the better. The individual alphabetical card system is the best, filing arrangements being a matter of personal choice and convenience. It is usual to keep separate the cards for male and female employees, and to make a similar distinction between past and present members. Cards should be filed in wooden, metal or strong cardboard containers, and preferably kept locked in the safe.

Among the particulars that should appear are: (a) full name, address, age, full name and address of wife or husband as the case may be, and number of children (if any); (b) wages and all increases, with dates; (c) overtime agreement; (d) whether agreement signed, and date; (e) national insurance registered number; (f) P.A.Y.E. number or code number; (g) references from last employer, if applied for; (h) date of leaving your employment, and reason; (i) name and address of new employer (if known) and whether reference given.

The work involved is justified by the information these cards yield. From them can be prepared figures of labour turnover, and also an analysis of the reasons for leaving, which are often most instructive.

It is quite a general practice to-day for payment of weekly wages to be made a few days after the close of the usual working week. For example, the week may end on a Tuesday and payment may be made on the Friday of that week, thus allowing the wages department to make up the wages after due checking of time-cards, etc., overtime and all the various deductions that have to be made in these times. Wages earned during these days of the week are termed as "lying time", and should the employee leave before the next usual pay day, this sum will be handed over to him.

P.A.Y.E.

Taxable pay means wages, salary, fees, overtime, commission, pension, holiday pay and payments made in lieu of benefits in kind, e.g. board wages. The following benefits in kind are usually treated as not taxable: free board and lodging, free supplies of coal, rent-free houses that particular employees are required to occupy.

Tax-deduction cards are of three kinds: weekly, monthly and emergency. In the main they are issued by the inspector of taxes, but an employer may prepare and use a fresh card for any new employee. The cards indicate Code No., or S.R. (Standard Rate), or N.T. (Not Taxable). No employer may alter a code number without advice from the inspector of taxes. The appropriate tax table—weekly or monthly—must be used for the week or month in which *payment* is made, irrespective of the period during which remuneration has been earned. All tax deducted must be from the *gross* sum due.

Supplies of necessary forms can be readily obtained from the local tax office, as can any assistance or advice. Always keep a stock of P.45 forms, which must be filled up whenever an employee leaves your service.

NATIONAL INSURANCE ACT, 1946

Classification is: (*a*) employed persons: (*b*) self-employed persons; and (*c*) non-employed persons. Age is from sixteen (school leaving age) to sixty-five for men, and sixteen to sixty for women. Ordinarily there are four types of card: boys under eighteen; girls under eighteen; men from eighteen to sixty-five; women from eighteen to sixty. Special cards are available for men over sixty-five and women over sixty who continue earning.

The total weekly payments now include contributions towards the Government graduated pension scheme and vary between 36s. 8d. (employee 19s. 4d.; employer 17s. 4d.) and 21s. (employee 11s. 2d.; employer 9s. 10d.). Firms which have their own pension schemes can, in certain circumstances, contract out of the Government scheme, thus reducing the weekly insurance payments. A helpful guide to national insurance is published by the

Government and can be obtained, price 9d., from H.M. Stationery Offices or any bookseller.

It is the employer's responsibility to stamp the cards, the employees' proportion being deducted from their wages or salary. Even if the employee works only one day in that week, the employer must stamp his card. Failure to pay contributions and to stamp cards incurs a liability for a maximum fine of ten pounds.

Nationality makes no distinction; contributions must be paid by every employer. If he so desires, an employee can inspect his card, not more often than once a month. Should a card become lost, destroyed or defaced, or if, after the lapse of reasonable notice, an employee should fail to produce his card, an employer must obtain an emergency card, which is available for thirteen weeks.

When a stamp has been affixed to a card it must be dated in ink or, preferably, by means of a metallic die, but never by means of a rubber stamp or pencil. Stamps must *not* be removed from a card. Completed cards must be exchanged for new cards through the local office of national insurance. Upon termination of employment the employer must return the card to the employee and may demand a receipt for it.

Cards should always be kept in a safe. They can be insured against loss.

Caterers are reminded that when, during the busy season, they employ persons who do not ordinarily work, these become liable for insurance contribution. Married women usually obtain part exemption and pay fourpence per week (Industrial Injuries Insurance), the employer paying three shillings and elevenpence. Part-time employment is in the same category, except: (*a*) if less than four hours a week with one employer; or (*b*) if, when engaged on domestic or cleaning work, less than eight hours a week with one employer. In both instances contributions by both parties are due under the industrial injuries section.

If in any doubt consult the local national insurance office.

Although to-day everyone can obtain free medical and other services, it is the highest wisdom to arrange for a periodical examination of your staff by a doctor, chiropodist and dentist. Fitness begets efficiency and the cost of these services can be looked upon as an investment in a most valuable asset—your staff.

ACCIDENTS TO STAFF

All employers of ten or more persons are required to keep an accident register, to facilitate notice of any accident that may occur on the premises. Full details can be entered either by the injured person or by someone on his behalf, and this is taken as sufficient evidence to the employers under the Industrial Injuries (Claims and Payments) Regulations, 1948. Accident registers (B.I.510) in the approved form can be obtained from Her Majesty's Stationery Office. They should be preserved for at least three years after the date of the last entry.

In the event of injuries from accidents, the employee can claim benefit as a right under the industrial injuries scheme. He may, in addition, lodge a claim for damages from his employer, but, should he do so, a proportion of the benefits he receives are taken into account when assessing the amount of damages. Claims are valid within six years of the date of the accident.

A point to be carefully noted by all employers is that an employer can now no longer escape liability should the accident resulting in injury and even death be caused by the negligence of a fellow employee.

The Law Reform (Personal Injuries) Act, 1948, abolished the employer's defence of "common employment", consequently all employers are strongly advised to effect adequate insurance against this risk, which, as evidenced by recent awards in the courts, can be very considerable.

Employers should take all possible steps to prevent accidents and to deal swiftly with them when they occur. Bacon- and bread-slicing machines should be fitted with guards; particular attention should be paid to all floors, to obviate accidents on greasy and uneven surfaces; first-aid equipment should be installed at accessible points; the employer, his telephonist and any other appropriate member of the staff should know the telephone numbers of the fire brigade, police, ambulance service and the nearest doctor.

A few words can be appended on the matter of accidents to patrons: burns due to spilt soup, tea or coffee; cuts due to chipped or broken glassware; falls caused by a loose stair-rod, a worn carpet or an over-polished floor—these are some examples. The risks can all be covered by insurance, but in some cases, where the placing of liability is uncertain, it is advisable to settle the claim, provided, of course, that it is reasonable. This is preferable to getting involved in expensive legal actions. Much depends upon the position and nature of your business, but considerable harm can be caused by persons with grudges, real or fancied.

Some precautions to take are: never have unlighted or insufficiently lighted stairways, corridors, etc.; guard against defective floor coverings and loose stair-rods; condemn chipped, cracked or discoloured china and glass, and damaged cutlery such as forks with bent prongs; make sure that all furniture is in good and safe condition, for, apart from more serious accidents, splinters from chairs can so easily damage nylon stockings.

TREATMENT AND TRAINING OF NEW STAFF

First impressions go a long way, and forty-eight hours of a hostile atmosphere can wreck many a promising worker's chances of success. New employees should be considerately treated on arrival. They should be made to feel welcome and placed under the care, or at least near, someone who is fully experienced, and who has a well-developed understanding and patience. The best can be got out of new employees only by giving them a real opportunity to settle in unfamiliar surroundings with the feeling that their co-workers and supervisors are anxious to be helpful.

There is another side to this. At some time or other everyone hits a bad patch, and often there is the desire to confide in someone. Here is a chance for some responsible member of the staff, with deep experience in life and a broad understanding, to assist in the welfare of his or her fellows and in the smooth running of the establishment.

As regards training, there are now about 150 hotel schools and catering colleges distributed throughout Britain, at which young men and women can take full-time and part-time courses in hotel and catering subjects, including both craft courses for chefs, waiters, chambermaids, etc., and management courses. Alongside these are official apprenticeship schemes, whereby training is given while working in hotels and restaurants, with part-time attendance at a training college. Full details of these facilities can be obtained from the Hotel & Catering Institute, 24 Portman Square, London, W.1.

Organized training for catering work has become essential, and the old system, whereby newcomers were thrown into jobs with practically no advice or instruction, cannot be too strongly condemned. It was one of the main causes of the high and costly labour turnover from which the industry has suffered so much.

STAFF UNIFORMS

It is now accepted in the industry that female workers are provided with mob-caps and overalls or some similar covering. For those in the kitchens and service-rooms white is preferable, although green is often useful in kitchens. Should you be running a snack-bar or similar establishment a primrose or pale pink shade is popular, or even a light shade of blue, but much depends upon your general colour scheme. No matter what colour you choose make quite certain that all female staff look their best in well-tailored garments. Looking good makes one feel good, and a becoming overall and cap have a moral uplift.

Waitresses in hotels often provide their own frocks, usually black, while the proprietor provides the aprons, cuffs, collar and frilly cap. In recent years many waitresses have appeared in neatly tailored overalls matching the general scheme. These are laundered free.

It is usual for all waiters to provide their own outfits, and the same for chefs, except that their trousers, tunic, hat and neckerchief are laundered at the expense of the proprietor. Uniforms as such are usually worn by door-men, hall-porters, lift attendants, etc. Provided the employer is satisfied that the holders of these posts are likely to remain in his employment, he should supply uniforms. A well-fitting uniform enhances the prestige of the establishment and raises the morale of the wearer. Colours are varied to-day and are a matter for personal choice.

SALESMANSHIP

Excepting, perhaps, the suave pressure of wine butlers in high-class hotels and restaurants, little or nothing is done among the multitude of other establishments to induce patrons or guests to partake of other or additional refreshments. It is not proposed that high-pressure sales-manship should be introduced and thus immediately nullify the many valiant efforts that have been and are being made to encourage a higher standard of service all round. What seems to be required is a combination of efficient sales and services conducted by carefully chosen waiting and selling staff (the latter at the many small cafés and self-service establishments), who can successfully camouflage sheer selling with interested and individual service.

WAITERS AND THEIR DUTIES

Maître d'Hôtel.—He is responsible for the entire organization of the dining-room and must be answerable direct to the general manager.

Reception Head Waiter.—He receives all patrons and allots them tables or conducts them to tables already reserved. He sees that they are comfortably seated and hands over the menu. If apéritifs or cocktails are desired he will call the wine waiter.

Station Head Waiters.—Their duties are similar to the foregoing, but they take the food orders. Usually they are in charge of a section comprising two stations.

Table Waiter or Chef de Rang.—He is responsible for the actual table service of all food dishes. Prior to the service he will lay his tables and attend to all condiments, linen, etc. required.

Lounge Waiter.—He works in the foyers or lounges, which it is usually a part of his duties to keep clean, polishing furniture, etc. He serves liquor of all kinds, afternoon teas, and coffee after luncheon and dinner.

Banquet Waiter.—He carries out general duties in the banqueting or functions department. His is often part-time employment.

Floor Waiter.—He is responsible for service of meals, etc. in private suites and bedrooms.

Commis Waiter.—He is an assistant waiter or what may be termed an apprentice. His work usually consists of dusting and sweeping; bringing into the dining-rooms all necessary supplies of crockery and cutlery; preparing cruets and stocking up sideboards and/or dumb-waiters. During the service of meals he acts as runner for his waiter, and thus gradually learns all the vital details of perfect service. He is often described as a Commis de Rang. To obtain additional experience he often serves for a period as Commis de Vins, acting as an assistant to the wine butler. His duties are to wash, dry and polish all glasses, and generally set up the wine table or trolley with glasses, ice bucket, salvers, etc. He also acts as runner for the wine butler, thereby learning all about wines and their correct service.

CHAPTER VI

**The Importance of Book-keeping—Small Caterer's
Financial Records—Summary Book of Goods Sold—
Cash Book—Petty Cash Book—Wages Book—Staff Time
Book—Purchase Day-book—Purchase Ledger—General
Ledger—Trial Balance**

DEALING as they do with financial records and the organization and control of catering concerns, this and the two
following chapters are of great importance and should be
carefully studied.

In this and the next chapter we consider the refresh-
ment-supplying establishment as distinct from the inn or
hotel, which provides in addition accommodation for
residential guests. It follows that a small business does
not call for such an elaborate system as does a larger
undertaking, yet there are certain fundamentals common
to them both.

THE IMPORTANCE OF BOOK-KEEPING

Apart from the fact that every owner, partner, executive
or director should know from time to time exactly how
the business stands, full, accurate and up-to-date financial
records and properly audited accounts are imperative
for:—

1. Obtaining correct assessment of income tax and
claiming wear-and-tear allowances.

2. Submission to bankers or financial corporations,
should their assistance be required.

3. Producing to prospective purchasers, should it be
desired to dispose of the business. Audited accounts
for at least five years may be called for.

4. Guidance of the owner or owners. Success of a

business can be measured only if it: (*a*) earns reasonable interest on the capital invested; (*b*) provides all owners and executives with remuneration at least equal to that which they could earn outside; and (*c*) provides a margin to meet foreseeable contingencies.

Book-keeping can be defined as the science and art of accurately recording in the appropriate books of account every business transaction that involves the transfer of money and/or goods and service. The correct system is that of double entry, where every single transaction involving the receiving and giving of money, goods and services requires to be recorded twice—that is to say, every debit must have a credit and every credit must have a debit entry. It provides a permanent record of all business transactions, whether these are of a personal or impersonal nature—that is, whether they concern persons or things such as cash, goods and running expenses. As each entry is twofold, arithmetical accuracy is attained. At the end of any period the combined effect of all transactions shows the financial position as set out by the trading account, the profit and loss account, and the balance sheet.

The following brief definitions may prove helpful:—

1. The debit side of an account is on the left; the credit side, on the right. In double-entry book-keeping the account that receives is *debited*, and the account that gives is *credited*.

2. Assets are the property or possessions of a business. These may be: (*a*) liquid, i.e. cash at bank; (*b*) floating, i.e. stock; (*c*) fixed, i.e. buildings, plant, etc.; (*d*) fictitious, i.e. goodwill.

3. Liabilities are sums owing.

4. Income or revenue is that which is derived from sales and/or services.

5. Expenses are such costs as are incurred in running

a business of any kind: wages, rent, insurance, travelling, power, heating, lighting, etc.

6. Profit may be gross or net. Gross profit is the excess of sales over purchases, after allowing for stock. Net profit is the balance of gross profit left over after payment of and provision for all expenses incurred in running the business. Gross and net loss are the reverse.

7. Turnover means total sales made during a given period.

8. Capital is generally the excess of assets over liabilities. It may be denoted as follows: (*a*) fixed, i.e. all fixed assets such as buildings, plant, etc.; (*b*) floating or circulating, i.e. cash, sundry debtors, stock; (*c*) loan, i.e. money borrowed on mortgage; (*d*) working, i.e. balance available after purchase price has been paid.

9 Discount may be trade or cash. Trade discount is a deduction made on the invoice, the purchaser being allowed a percentage of the listed price—ten, twenty or twenty-five per cent, according to the custom of the particular trade. Cash discount is an allowance made for prompt payment.

Primarily, book-keeping records should classify and analyse *all* transactions over a period, and the final result should set out:—

1. Totals of purchases and sales, classified if desired.

2. Totals of amounts expended or incurred under every desired heading of expense.

3. Amount and nature of all assets and liabilities.

4. Amount of net profit or loss.

5. Amount of capital.

Books of account can be divided into two classes:—

Books of Prime Entry

These are the subsidiary books in which entries are

made before being posted to the books of final entry, i.e. the ledgers.   They include:—

(*a*) Cash Book, in which are recorded all sums paid and received in cash or through the bank.   In large concerns it is more convenient to have two books: Cash Paid and Cash Received.

(*b*) Petty Cash Book, in which are recorded minor items of cash expenditure or receipt.

(*c*) Purchase Day-book, in which are recorded all purchases other than cash purchases.

(*d*) Sales Day-book, in which are recorded all sales other than cash sales.

(*e*) Journal, in which are recorded all miscellaneous entries that cannot go directly into the ledger from any other of the books of prime entry.

Books of Final Entry

These are the ledgers in which all the debits and credits from the books of prime entry are posted under such headings as may be decided upon.   They include :—

(*a*) Purchase Ledger, in which are kept the personal accounts of trade creditors, and to which are posted the entries from the purchase day-book.

(*b*) Sales (or Sundry Debtors) Ledger, in which are kept the personal accounts of customers, and to which are posted the entries from the sales day-book.

(*c*) General Ledger, in which are kept all impersonal accounts of expense or income: property, rent, rates, wages, profit and loss, etc.   Frequently kept distinct from the general ledger is:—

(*d*) Private Ledger, in which are kept all accounts of a confidential nature: capital accounts of the company, partnership or individual concern; accounts of all assets such as buildings, plant, equipment, good-will, furniture, fixtures and fittings: motor vehicles, investments, stocks, liabilities, mortgages, loans, etc.; accounts recording depreciation, and directors' salaries and fees; dividends and interest received and paid; and the profit and loss accounts. This private ledger is always kept in the safe and often has a small lock fitted to it.

A system of book-keeping suitable for the large establishment is described in Chapter VIII. Here we can confine ourselves to the financial records that should be kept by the smaller caterer.

SMALL CATERER'S FINANCIAL RECORDS

However restricted your premises, it is wise to have at least a corner in which to place a desk, or table with drawers, equipped with the usual stationery. Purchase the necessary files for storing invoices, receipts and correspondence. Invoices may be filed in order of date, and by the name of the firm supplying; receipts in order of date of payment; correspondence in date order and under the name of the person or firm, or of a specific subject.

A safe is most essential. In it should be placed all records and books of account, national insurance cards, unbanked cash takings, and cash for purchases and petty expenses. Should you have any deeds, insurance policies, etc., these can be deposited for safe custody with your bank or solicitor.

Essential books of account are:—

1. Summary Books of Goods Sold
2. Cash Book
3. Petty Cash Book
4. Wages Book
5. Staff Time Book
6. Purchase Day-book
7. Purchase Ledger
8. General Ledger.

If these are written up regularly week by week, and a bank reconciliation prepared, the professional accountant will be in a position to prepare final accounts for the period under review with some degree of confidence and without undue delay.

Business being mainly on a cash basis the small caterer will not normally require a sales day-book or a sales ledger.

Summary Book of Goods Sold

This is an analysed record of receipts from all sources and is posted weekly from the daily summary prepared by the cashier (see A CHECKING SYSTEM, page 108). The totals of the various columns of the daily summary are posted daily to the cash book.

Cash Book

On the *debit* side are posted in columnar form the totals from the daily summary, together with any other cash received. On the *credit* are total columns for sums: (*a*) paid out in cash; (*b*) paid by cheque; and (*c*) lodged in the bank. These are followed by analysis columns for the various outlays such as food purchases, cleaning materials, wages and national insurance, heating and lighting, rent and rates, general expenses, printing, stationery and postages, purchases of utensils and equipment, and, finally, a Private column. All cash received each day should be banked the following day, and thus each day's total as shown in the cash book should equal the amount shown on the pay-in slip and credited on the bank pass-sheet.

On the appropriate day for payment of all monthly accounts, cheques are made out and entered in detail in the cash book, then posted therefrom to the various accounts in the purchase ledger. Any discount should be entered in a separate column in the cash book and similarly posted. In a number of establishments it is customary to enter invoices net, but it is worth any extra work to show cash discounts separately in the cash book and purchase ledger, as these figures really represent an allowance for prompt payment and help to meet the cost of overheads.

At regular periods, preferably monthly, the total of the debit column in the cash book should be posted to the credit of the appropriate account in the general ledger.

It may be of interest to small caterers that there is on the market an excellent all-in-one cash book that meets the normal needs of most businesses and can even dispense with a petty cash book. It is admirably suited for those desiring weekly results, as each opening covers requirements for one week, and at the end are pages set apart for cumulative purposes. The price is 17s. 6d. and is money well spent.

Petty Cash Book

This usually has a cash column on the left-hand or debit side for the record of cash received. Farther to the right is a total-payment column preceded by columns for the date and details. Beyond the total-payment column are various analysis columns for the expenses incurred.

It is advisable to keep the petty cash on the imprest system: advancing from the main cash a sum of, say, £25 and at the end of each week or month reimbursing the exact amount spent, e.g. £21 14s. 9d. At the end of each week or month as desired, the book should be balanced, ruled off and the totals of the various columns posted to the appropriate accounts in the general ledger.

Blocks of petty-cash vouchers should be purchased in two colours—one for supplies and the other for expenses. This saves time when entering up the book. Insist on a receipt for every payment, however small it may be.

Wages Book

In this should appear the names of all employees and, if a time clock is used, their numbers. If the size of staff warrants it, divisions into departments or sections is advised, as this will provide valuable information for costing.

Rulings in addition to number and name can be: rate of weekly or hourly pay; number of hours worked each day; amount of pay, overtime, and gross amount; deductions for national insurance, P.A.Y.E., savings, pensions, etc.; net sum due; and a column for employer's proportion of national insurance.

It is advisable to draw a cheque to cover net sum to be paid; another for national insurance stamps; and, each month, a cheque in favour of the Inland Revenue for P.A.Y.E. deducted. Details of the cheques should be entered on the credit side of the cash book, and posted to the analysed columns on the debit side of the wages/salaries account in the general ledger.

Where the number of executives warrants it, keep a salaries book. Separate cheques should be drawn for net salaries, which are usually paid monthly, national insurance and P.A.Y.E. If the sums involved do not justify this course, these payments can easily be amalgamated with those drawn in the wages section.

Unless the establishment is comparatively small and the number of employees few, it is advisable to adopt one of the modern wage-recording systems on loose sheets. The top copy is perforated into strips, each of which when torn off gives the worker the fullest details of how his pay is made up, while the carbon copy is placed in a binder as a permanent record.

Staff Time Book

The keeping of this has a moral effect, and is useful for future reference.

Purchase Day-book

This should be columnar: date; name of supplier; invoice number(s); posting folio; total; analysis columns.

These last can include: groceries and provisions; meat, fish and poultry; vegetables and fruit; tinned goods; cigarettes and tobacco; fuel, electricity and gas; laundry and cleaning; repairs, renewals and replacements—subdivided into buildings, plant and equipment, furniture, fittings and fixtures, china and glass, cutlery, linen; and, finally, a general column. If required, suitable columns can be added for wines and spirits, beer, cider and minerals.

This book should be written up, preferably daily, from invoices, all of which have been duly passed by someone in authority, fully checked with the copies of the original orders, the delivery notes and the goods-received book, which last is referred to in the next chapter.

If they are not too numerous, credit notes received for goods returned, over-charges, and containers returned can be recorded in a section of the purchase day-book, preferably at the back of it. It is usually necessary, however, to have a returns or allowances book for this purpose.

When deliveries of, for instance, milk, bread and rolls, vegetables and fish are made daily or more frequently, time and space can be saved by filing the invoices until the end of each week or month, tabulating them, and making only one weekly or monthly entry in the purchase day-book. Each invoice or batch should be consecutively numbered month by month and carefully filed for future reference and scrutiny by auditors.

The purchase day-book should be cast and cross-cast each month. The individual entries will, of course, be posted to the credit side of the various suppliers' accounts in the purchase ledger, the total to the credit side of the sundry-creditors account in the general or private ledger, and the totals of the respective analysis columns debited to the appropriate accounts in the same ledger, thus completing the double entry.

Purchase Ledger

The purpose of this has already been explained. It should be balanced monthly.

General Ledger

This is the permanent record of all accounts posted from the books of prime entry. It also should be balanced monthly. In it should be a control account for the purchase ledger, reflecting collectively the details of that ledger, so that the general ledger can be self-contained.

It is usual, at the end of each month or other period, to prepare a trial balance, which is a list of all accounts in the general ledger having a balance. The balances remaining on the purchase ledger are usually listed separately, and balanced with the aid of the control account in the general ledger.

A trial balance, it should be noted, proves only the arithmetical accuracy of the book-keeping. It does not reveal: (a) compensating errors; (b) total omissions; (c) mispostings of amounts or errors of commission; or (d) errors of principle.

Matters relating to the trading account, the profit and loss account and the balance sheet have a wider application to the catering business as a whole, so can be suitably deferred until Chapter VIII.

CHAPTER VII

Internal Control—Buying Supplies—Conserving Food—
Extermination of Vermin—Estimating Food Cost—
Regulating Portions—Relating Costs to Turnover—A
Checking System—The Selling Side—Additional
Sources of Profit—Advertising—Trade Publications and
the Catering Exhibition

INTERNAL CONTROL

THE present-day value in cash of food and drink is so
high that it is imperative that an efficient system of internal
control be installed and permanently maintained, to ensure
that the fullest return is received from all commodities
sold and all services rendered. In addition, there is the
moral responsibility on all owners and executives to
eliminate or at least reduce to an absolute minimum all
scope for pilfering and defalcation by employees.

The extent of control is contingent upon the size of the
establishment. Where the owner is more or less in
constant attendance and can keep a strict eye on the
general operations, this may prove sufficient. Generally
speaking, however, some measure of control is essential
in most establishments. Size and importance of the
undertaking will largely determine the system required
and the manner in which it is operated. It should be noted
that any system installed must suit the requirements of the
business; never must business be moulded to the system.
Once installed, the system must work continuously and
to its fullest capacity. There must never be any slackness;
staff are only too quick to notice loopholes and take full
advantage of them.

In practice control and costing are, or should be, com-
plementary. Every item of expenditure should be carefully analysed; every side of the business studied, from
buying supplies to advertising in the local press.

BUYING SUPPLIES

Wherever the premises are and whatever the class of
patron, certain fundamentals must be observed in the
running of restaurants, tea-rooms and the like. It should
never be forgotten that in this class of business, owing to
the perishable nature of the stock, practically the complete
cycle is accomplished in one day. Raw materials are
purchased in the morning, converted by preparation and
cooking into saleable articles at lunch-time and tea-time
and for any evening trade, then the takings are placed in
the night safe of the bank.

This rapidity of action makes imperative a system of
sound organization. The difference between profit and
loss on the business of any one day, and even on a particular
dish, is frequently so small that haphazard methods, errors
in buying, waste, erratic portioning or faulty administration, may easily result in heavy losses and consequent
disaster. All food represents money spent, and every
effort should be made to ensure an adequate return from its
preparation and sale.

So often the small caterer is lax when placing orders for
supplies. He is probably well known to his suppliers,
particularly to those giving deliveries of milk, bread and
rolls, vegetables, etc., and this daily contact breeds a
familiarity that dispenses with such important records as
invoices. Some day a dispute may lead to broken relations,
both business and personal.

All orders should be in writing, made out in a duplicate
book with numbered pages, the top copies only being
perforated. Verbal orders, direct or by telephone, should
be confirmed in writing. The carbon copies remaining
fast in the order book will enable the caterer to check all
deliveries against either a delivery note or an invoice, or a
record kept by him in a goods-received (or goods-inwards)

book or pad, the pages of which are also numbered and in duplicate. In fact, it is an excellent plan to enter all deliveries in this book, even those accompanied by a delivery note or invoice.

Wherever possible arrange for all goods to be delivered at the back or goods entrance, thus avoiding transport men parading at all hours through the restaurant with milk, bread, sacks of potatoes and large cartons. Appoint some member of the staff to receive the goods and make a quick check of them before signing. The top copy of the goods-received note should accompany the consignment to whatever section or department of the establishment it is taken.

Arrange for daily deliveries of all perishables such as milk, bread and rolls, vegetables, fish and even meat. It is also a good plan to settle the accounts at short intervals—daily or weekly. It does not involve much work and means that you are on good terms with your suppliers, and that cash remaining at the end of the week, assuming that you have no large bills outstanding, can be earmarked for settling rent, rates, gas, electricity, and replacements.

Buying demands constant study as to quantity required, quality, prices ruling, quantity of stock in hand, and anticipated needs. It is infinitely better to have a comparatively short menu, changed daily, than a full one calling for larger purchases and probably heavier stocks, besides leading to more work in the kitchen, more cluttering up of the hot-plate, more left-overs and consequently more made-up dishes on the following day. It also wastes the time of your service-room and waiting staffs while patrons browse through a menu that resembles a sale catalogue. Shorter menus mean fewer left-overs and make for frequent changes in your daily fare—in a word: variety.

Unless the employer is in a position to attend to the buying, it should be placed in the hands of some person who is not only fully qualified, but also scrupulously honest. As a preliminary to placing orders, investigation should be made into the actual consumption over a period of, say, six months, with due allowance for seasonal and other fluctuations. Only after careful consideration, and inquiries as to terms and deliveries, should firm orders be placed.

Endeavour to co-operate with your suppliers in the matter of regular ordering, avoiding as far as possible urgent demands for deliveries. Remember to offer the odd cigarette or cup of tea or coffee to the delivery staffs. These human touches pay dividends far in excess of their intrinsic value.

In some areas, outside of large cities, local caterers should get together and form a centralized buying committee. The saving to be derived from bulk buying, and the economies effected in transport and packing charges, will offset any cost of specialized buyers.

CONSERVING FOOD

Enlist the co-operation of your chef or female cook and, if you employ one, your storeman. They should see that all goods are invoiced correctly and that quality, quantity and price are fully checked on arrival. Instil into your chef or cook the urgent and constant need of economy in handling all food, every ounce of which represents cash. Your expected profit on particular dishes may have vanished before they have been served in the restaurant or dining-room. From a practical standpoint it is frequently not easy, but insist on your chef or cook working daily and every day to recognized recipes. So often there is a complete lack of method in the preparation of dishes.

As meat is the food item of greatest cost, carefully consider the merits of, say, mutton against pork when roasted, or an ordinary joint against meat boned and rolled. Watch

D

joints for excessive fat or suet charged at the same rate per pound as the meat. Study loss in weight due to preparation and to roasting or boiling, as the case may be. See that all roasting is done at the correct temperature. Three hundred degrees is recommended; four hundred may mean up to fifty per cent more loss. Use aluminium skewers, which are first-class conductors of heat. Always weigh every delivery of meat, fish and poultry.

Install a refrigerator of a suitable size, keep it spotlessly clean and use it to store all your fats, fish, meat (fresh or cooked) and left-overs. It will quickly repay its cost. Install all possible labour-saving devices: washing-up machine, can-opener, bread- and bacon-slicing machines, butter-pat machine, electric potato-peeler, graded servers for mashed potatoes and ice cream, standard soup-ladles. Experience will suggest others.

Provide an airy cupboard for all cereals, tinned goods, etc., and keep it locked. Pilfering, even on a small scale, eats into profits, and this is not always confined to raw and prepared foods, but to surreptitious hiding of odd items during the busy periods of the day—a few pats of butter, a sardine or two, a couple of rolls, some left-over meat patties, and so on. "Empty" milk-churns are often receptacles for carrying out tinned food and other plunder.

Every evening examine the garbage and swill bins. Their contents may surprise you. So many cooks have a preference for these instead of the stock-pot, where the prime elements of soups, sauces, gravies, etc. are created, and real profit can be made.

Arrange for daily issues of stores at fixed hours—for example, at 8 a.m. and 4 p.m.—by either yourself or your cashier. Instruct all those who require stores to make out written chits in duplicate, top copies to be held by the person issuing the stores, carbon copies remaining fast in the book for any future check or reference.

EXTERMINATION OF VERMIN

Enforce strict cleanliness in every department, for carelessness encourages all types of vermin—rats, mice, cockroaches, etc.—and thereby causes, through depreciation, waste of food and other stores. This not only costs money, but also may easily lead to poisoned food being served to patrons.

Institute a real war against these pests. Have your building thoroughly surveyed by someone competent, so that all structural defects that encourage vermin to enter and multiply are rectified. Block up every hole with cement and glass. Use covered bins for kitchen swill and garbage. See that the latter are emptied at least twice a day and, if into an outside depository, that this too is pest-proof. Vegetables containers, placed several inches above floor level, should be solid at the bottom and at least one third of the way up the sides.

No food, either raw or prepared, should be left around in dishes, saucepans, etc., after the day's business is over. It should be placed in the refrigerator or cold store, or on the highest point of the range if need be.

If, having done all these things, you are still at times plagued, arrange for the services of a reputable and nationally known pest-extermination organization, which will pay regular visits at a cost infinitesimal compared with the risk you run by neglect.

ESTIMATING FOOD COST

Prepare each week a summary of goods consumed. Divide the sheet into ten cash columns (eleven if you open on Sundays), allowing sufficient space to the left of the first column for a list of all the relative items: milk, bread, fats, fish, meat, vegetables, fruit, tinned goods, groceries,

SUMMARY OF GOODS CONSUMED

Week Ending ....

Commodity	Stock in Hand, br. fwd.	Net Purchases and Supplies from Store							Total	Less Stock in Hand	Total Consumption	Percentage
		Monday	Tuesday	Wednesday	Thursday	Friday	Saturday	Sunday				
				IF REQUIRED								
Meat: Beef												
Mutton												
Pork												
Fish: Sole												
Plaice												
Turbot												
Cod												
Potatoes												
Peas: Tinned												
Frozen												
Margarine												
Flour												

etc. Pricing all the items at cost, complete the first cash column by writing in the value of the stock in hand of each item at the beginning of the week—that is to say, perishables left over from the previous week, and the residue of goods issued during the previous week from the store-cupboard. By casting up these figures you will arrive at the total of the opening stock.

The next six (or seven) columns cover the days of the week. In them should be entered the value of the perishables delivered (less returns), plus all goods issued from the store cupboard. The total of each daily column will give the cost of all purchases and issues on that day and the next column the total for the week of each item. The next column is for the value of the stock of each item in hand at the close of the week. To arrive at the food costs for the week, subtract the totals in the last column from the sum of the totals of the other columns, i.e. usage is represented by the total of the opening stock and all purchases and issues, less the closing stock.

By using the weekly summary of goods consumed in conjunction with the weekly summary of goods sold (see page 110), you can work out percentages of food costs per total, and also against the various classes of dishes. Fluctuations are bound to occur, when, for instance, new vegetables and fruit come on the market, or when, at certain seasons, patrons will expect various other items to appear on your menu, even though the cost of them is high. At these times you must use ingenuity and judicious buying to level out the effects of the higher prices you have had to pay for these seasonal foods.

Success in the industry largely depends upon the keeping of a close watch on food cost, which represents the largest percentage of costs. Every week carefully consider the results as shown by the summary of goods consumed and the summary of goods sold, and investigate all material differences, which may be due to: (a) paying too high

Commodities	Stock in Hand, br. fwd.	Goods Received and Issues from Store.				
		Monday	Tuesday	Wednesday	Thursday	Frid
Meat:						
Beef . . .	2 4 6	4 5 6	— — —	3 19 —	— — —	—
Mutton . .	1 3 —	— — —	4 9 6	— — —	4 3 6	—
Pork . .	1 — —	— — —	— — —	— — —	— — —	3 18
Fish:						
Plaice . .	— — —	— — —	2 17 6	— — —	— — —	3 —
Haddock . .	— — —	— — —	— — —	1 19 —	— — —	
Cod . .	— — —	1 2 6	— — —	— — —	2 7 6	1 7
Vegetables:						
Potatoes . .	2 9 —	5 — —	— — —	5 — —	— — —	5 —
Cabbage . .	— — —	10 —	— — —	— — —	12 6	
Cauliflower .	— — —	— — —	15 3	— — —	— — —	12
Peas (tinned) .	9 —	12 —	— — —	15 —	— — —	12
Baked Beans (tinned)	13 —	— — —	1 — —	— — —	15 —	
Fats:						
Butter . .	7 6	10 —	— — —	10 —	— — —	1
Margarine .	10 9	1 — —	— — —	1 — —	10 —	
Cooking (Lard) .	5 3	15 —	— — —	15 —	10 —	—
Groceries:						
Flour . .	7 9	14 —	— — —	1 1 —	— — —	1
Custard Powder .	4 6	— — —	10 6	— — —	— — —	1
Rice . .	3 —	— — —	9 —	— — —	— — —	
Spaghetti . .	3 9	— — —	— — —	7 6	— — —	
Marmalade .	2 3	— — —	6 9	— — —	— — —	
Fruits:						
Apples . .	4 —	— — —	1 5 —	— — —	— — —	1
Bananas . .	— — —	— — —	— — —	19 —	— — —	14
Pears (tinned) .	10 6	1 7 6	— — —	— — —	17 6	
Apricots (tinned) .	7 3	— — —	14 —	— — —	— — —	1
Milk . .	— — —	1 5 —	1 — —	1 10 —	1 — —	1 1
Bread . .	— — —	17 6	15 —	1 7 6	1 5 —	1
Totals . .	£10 5 —	17 19 —	14 2 6	19 3 —	12 . 1 . —	22 1

NOTE: Assuming Takings of £270 for the week; the percentage costs are as set out in
listed would give approximately a 40% Food C

SUMMARY (*In Value*)

Week Ending:		Total for Week	Deduct Stock in Hand	Consumption for Week	Classification Totals	Percentage of Sales
Saturday	Sunday					
4 - -		14 9 -	1 5 6	13 3 6	} 25 15 6	9·54
- - -		9 16 -	17 -	8 19 -		
- - -		3 18 6	5 6	3 13 -		
- -		5 17 6	- - -	5 17 6	} 13 3 6	4·89
10 -		2 9 -	- - -	2 9 -		
4 17 -		4 17 -	- - -	4 17 -		
- -		17 9 -	4 - -	13 9 -	} 20 1 3	7·43
5 -		1 7 6	6 -	1 7 6		
- -		1 7 9	- - -	1 7 9		
- -		2 8 -	17 -	1 11 -		
12 6		3 - 6	14 6	2 6 -		
- - -		2 2 6	7 -	1 15 6	} 6 19 9	2·59
10 -		3 10 9	10 9	3 - -		
7 6		2 12 9	8 6	2 4 3		
- - -		3 3 9	14 -	2 9 9	} 6 1 3	2·24
- - -		1 16 -	8 -	1 8 -		
- - -		1 1 -	4 6	16 6		
- - -		18 9	3 -	15 9		
- - -		15 9	4 6	11 3		
- - -		2 4 -	7 -	1 17 -	} 6 19 -	2·59
- - -		1 9 -	- - -	1 9 -		
- - -		2 15 6	14 -	2 1 6		
- - -		1 18 9	7 3	1 11 6		
1 - -		7 5 -	- - -	7 5 -	7 5 -	2·69
17 6		5 17 6	- - -	5 17 6	5 17 6	2·16
8 2 6		104 10 9	12 8 -	92 2 9	92 2 9	34·13

Sunday column (vertical): IF REQUIRED

column: adding cost of Tea, Coffee, etc., used, plus other commodities not
Values shown are hypothetical.

prices; (b) selling at too low prices; (c) buying food of such low quality that, owing to wastage in preparation, etc., it costs more than food of a higher quality; (d) bad handling in the kitchen—faulty preparation of vegetables and fruits, over-cooking, under-cooking, bad handling of fish and meat prior to cooking, wrong carving, etc.; (e) portions too large and unappetizingly presented to patrons: (f) pilfering; (g) failure to utilize all left-overs, which can give good profit and tasty dishes the next day.

A continuously high food cost means a speedy journey to bankruptcy; a low food cost means that you are robbing your patrons. Aim at a food cost of forty per cent of your drawings, leaving a sixty per cent gross profit to meet all running expenses. Seasonal fluctuations in prices may cause the food cost to rise or fall a little, but endeavour should be made to keep it as steady as possible.

When costing a meal or just a dish, be sure to include every expense involved. Take into account not only the food, but also its preparation and service: staff costs such as wages, salaries, food and accommodation, national insurance, pensions contributions, uniforms, holidays with pay, etc.; all overhead expenses such as rent, rates, fuel, cleaning materials, etc. Each meal and each dish must bear its proportionate share of all these items, which have to be paid for and consequently must be taken into full account. For example, your rent and rates may cost you, say, £300 p.a., which is roughly £1 per working day. Should you serve two hundred and fifty meals a day, you must add a penny to the cost of each one served.

REGULATING PORTIONS

When we pay for twenty cigarettes we expect to receive twenty in the packet. We should protest if we found only eighteen and would be surprised if the packet contained twenty-two. But every day in the catering business, patrons get that extra portion of potatoes, another roll, or a more expensive vegetable than the one that should accompany a particular dish. Seldom are any of these charged to the patron, especially if he is generous with his tips. So often a waitress will ask for " a little more for Mr X ", yet that little more may easily eat up the small margin of profit on the whole meal.

To regulate portions, first ascertain the exact inclusive cost of each item, be it a sirloin of beef, a roast chicken or simply half a hundredweight of mashed potatoes, taking into account cost of raw material, unavoidable loss due to preparation, shrinkage, etc., all costs of preparation, cooking and serving, plus a fair proportion of your overheads. Then ascertain the number of reasonable portions you can anticipate, bearing in mind a forty per cent food cost, add your profit and thus arrive at the selling price.

Consult your chef, service-room assistants and waiting staff in this matter of size of portions and when it has been decided upon, endeavour to get everyone to adhere rigidly to the prescribed quantities, unless special circumstances intervene. You are bound to receive complaints, but these are often from one per cent or less of your patrons and, while they are upsetting at the time, they can be countered by giving a little extra as a special concession. Better to give one additional portion to satisfy a complaint than to give all patrons portions in excess of what you can really afford, and for which they are not paying. Be fair to them and just to yourself.

Circumstances may and do arise when speed of service is vital and the waiting staff may have to serve the portions themselves, but again strict observance of standard quantities must be demanded of them.

Always use the correct size of plate or dish for each course. A moderate portion can appear skimpy if served on a large plate. In this respect particular attention should be paid to ice-cream. To obtain the maximum number of portions, use the correct size of server, have it just filled and not overflowing, have the ice-cream at the proper serving temperature, and see that the person serving it is of the conscientious type and not heavy-handed.

Make constant "spot" checks of the cost of your various dishes, especially the good-selling ones. The serving of portions of regulated size and the elimination of all food waste, whether it is due to ignorance, carelessness in preparation or faulty cooking, are imperative in the attainment of success.

RELATING COSTS TO TURNOVER

To arrive at food cost and the gross rate of profit essential, analyse carefully the type of food sold and the rate of sale. Profit naturally varies with the commodity. The following are some samples, showing the average rate of gross profit:—

Meat dishes	.	.	.	.	.	48–50 per cent
Fish dishes	.	.	.	.	.	55–60 ,,
Vegetables and salads	.	.	.	.	55–60 ,,
Snacks, etc.	.	.	.	.	.	60–65 ,,
Sweets	.	.	.	.	.	65–70 ,,
Tea and coffee	.	.	.	.	.	70–75 ,,

The next step is to ascertain the proportion of each commodity sold every day or week, and therefrom calculate percentage yield. Much depends upon the class of business—whether it is, for example, a snack-bar, a combination of snack-bar and self-service café, or a restaurant with table service. Whichever it is, the relation of costs to the total turnover can be estimated by carefully setting out, under clear and comprehensive headings, the costs of running the business, then working out the percentage of each against your turnover.

As we have seen, food costs should be about forty per cent. Staff costs are governed by the size and type of the premises, but should be from twenty-four to thirty per cent. Overheads such as heating, lighting, cooking fuel, telephone and laundry will be largely controlled by the volume of business done, assuming that strict economy is exercised. If when to these have been added proportionate percentages to cover rent, rates and other expenses, and the balance remaining is not less than ten per cent, you are probably doing quite well, but if the net profit falls consistently below this figure, immediate investigation is called for. Of course, fluctuations are bound to occur, owing at times to outside influences, but if the results are low week after week, the outlook is not cheerful. Watch these percentages most keenly; they are the unfailingly accurate barometer of the condition of your little enterprise.

Profits can be boosted by: (a) increasing prices; (b) cutting costs; (c) increasing turnover without increasing costs out of proportion.

The first is rather a doubtful method and, unless backed by superior quality of food and impeccable service, is usually doomed to failure.

The second is much more commendable, for in every business there is always scope for reorganization, for trying out new methods and installing labour-saving devices. How many patrons should each waitress serve per day, giving them satisfactory attention and at the same time giving you full value for wages, etc., paid? Dispensing with even one employee, thereby saving five pounds a week, plus national insurance contributions, the cost of meals, overalls and maybe lodging, can make a big difference to your weekly results. Although the capital cost of labour-saving devices may appear high, especially for the smaller place, they lead to increased efficiency and an eventual saving in time, money and effort.

The third method is to gear your establishment by every known means to such a state of perfection that the public will patronize it because of good food justly priced and well and speedily served. With little extra cost, other than on food and cooking fuel, you may possibly serve one hundred and fifty meals at midday instead of a hundred as formerly. Volume of business ultimately determines the net profits. The greater value you give your patrons, the greater will be your turnover. Although the giving of good value may and does reduce the percentage of profit, this lower percentage is safe on a large and increasing turnover, because it is *volume* of profits that counts. Better to make seven and a half per cent on a turnover of £400 per week than ten per cent on £280 per week. While turnover is important it does not always mean profit. £1,000 net profit on an annual turnover of £10,000 is far preferable to a £100,000 turnover that may resolve itself into a £1,000 loss.

Never be afraid to face the actual costs of running your business. Accurately record all details, work out the weekly result, and then analyse the figures. If labour costs seem high, then see if the staff are slow, and whether the fault lies with the kitchen and service side or with the waiting section. By critical approach to every aspect of the business you will speedily find the cause of the trouble and, we trust, the correct solution.

A CHECKING SYSTEM

In the ordinary course check-pads are not required in snack-bars, cafeterias and other self-service establishments. Cash is paid before the patron commences his snack or meal, either to the counter assistant or to a cashier seated at the end of the service counter. In canteens the arrangements are much the same, but in most restaurants, tea-rooms and hotels, check-pads are essential.

Even if you have only one or two waitresses, install a checking system, which, although it may appear irksome to those concerned, does inculcate care in the ordering and charging to patrons of all dishes, and ensures to a large extent your receiving the correct payment for all beverages and dishes served.

For this purpose use an ordinary check-pad having a perforation near the top, but allowing sufficient space for the insertion of the total of the bill and the number of patrons served. Below are set out the items—soup, fish, meat and vegetables, sweets, tea, coffee, sandwiches, pastries, etc.—with the usual cash column. The pads normally consist of fifty or a hundred checks, which are numbered consecutively.

The best system is that in which there are two checks—a cash check and a supply check—for each order. The supply check, bearing the same number as the cash check, is either in the form of a perforated extension to it, or (as is more usual) is placed behind it. The cash check goes to the customer, the supply check to the kitchen, service-room, still-room, or (if the premises are licensed) dispense, for the various dishes and beverages required. To facilitate this the supply check is divided by perforations into five or six sections.

Each waiter or waitress should have distinct check-pads, the numbers on the checks being preceded by an identifying letter of the alphabet. A responsible person should be put in charge of all stock pads, which should be kept under lock. Record should be made of all supplies received and of all issues to the waiting staff, i.e. type of pad, starting and finishing numbers, to whom issued and date. Strict watch must be kept on all movements of these pads.

Instructions to the serving sections should be: " No service if no supply check." Immediately orders have been executed the various supply checks should be placed on spiked files, after being marked or defaced in some way to prevent duplication in favour of some regular customer who tips well in exchange for a free meal at the caterer's expense.

All bills handed to patrons should be sufficiently detailed to enable them to check each item with the menu, and also to enable the cashier to analyse the various items easily and accurately. In no circumstances should cash checks or supply checks be destroyed; where mistakes have occurred the checks should be marked " Cancelled " and bear the initials of the proprietor, supervisor or manageress as the case may be.

It is the duty of the cashier to collect all cash tendered, either by patrons or waitresses, in settlement of bills. She should be provided with a suitable float, made up of such variety of change as trade necessitates. This float should be checked at frequent but irregular intervals. The cash checks should be filed in numerical order; if the cashier finds there is one missing she should report the fact with all speed.

The cashier should use every spare moment in analysing the checks in a ruled note-book (the daily summary referred to on page 101), setting out on the left-hand side the numbers of the cash checks that have been presented, and, in the analysis columns, details in accordance with those given on the cash check; soup, fish, meat and vegetables, etc. The daily totals of the columns should be transferred at the close of business to the summary book of goods sold, which will, when cast, show the cash value of all food and drink disposed of during the week under review. The totals of the various sections of the daily summary should be posted daily to the cash book.

Examine the daily summary in conjunction with the supply checks handed in at the service, and endeavour to reconcile them. Always bear in mind the possibility of collusion between your waiting staff and patrons, between your cashier and patrons, and between your waiting staff and serving staff.

In establishments such as snack-bars, where cash is

usually paid direct to the assistant who serves the patron, additional care is necessary when engaging counter staff. Make certain that they are honest, and institute checks from time to time to satisfy yourself that correct prices are charged and that all cash received is properly registered and actually placed in the till or cash register. In canteens, unless there is a system of pre-purchase of tickets of various denominations from machines, the bulk of the receipts is also in cash. Here too there is a distinct possibility of collusion between canteen staff and workers.

THE SELLING SIDE

A soiled tablecloth, a full ashtray, yesterday's menu still on the table, stale mustard, empty pepper-pots, salt-cellars and sugar-bowls, badly washed cutlery and china—these are among the things that can injure existing business and future prospects. Each day that dawns provides a fresh opportunity to retain your present patrons and gain new ones.

Aim at such a standard in the working sections of your establishment that you will be able and proud to show your patrons round. Endeavour to build up a reputation for the consistent quality of your food, beverages and service. The public are critical—and rightly so—of the quality of tea and coffee served in places of refreshment.

Tea.—(a) Use good leaf; it gives better tea and more cups to the pound; (b) store properly, preferably in a lidded tea-chest raised by a few bricks to prevent dampness getting in, and kept away from strong odours such as soap, cheese, etc.; (c) use the correct quantity of leaf, freshly drawn boiling water and scrupulously clean vessels; (d) thoroughly warm tea-pot; (e) use short pour; (f) allow time to infuse or brew, but never allow it to stew; (g) tea and (if taken) milk and sugar should come together at the last possible moment.

Coffee.—(*a*) Arrange with your supplier for a blend suitable to local water and your patrons' taste; (*b*) make certain that your equipment is cleaned after each making; (*c*) never use detergents on the inner linings of your coffee urns; (*d*) ensure that all water used is fresh and boiling— no more; (*e*) accurately measure coffee and water; this is imperative to secure consistently good coffee; (*f*) serve it really hot; (*g*) never boil the liquid; (*h*) use cream when you can, but this should not be too heavy with butter fat.

Tea- and coffee-making are specialized jobs and should be entrusted only to trained staff who take a real pride in producing excellent beverages.

No matter whether yours is a restaurant in the city or a tea-house situated in some beauty spot, there are certain essentials. All floors should be thoroughly cleaned each day; all furniture dusted and polished; walls swept down regularly; lighting installations (so often neglected) polished; table-cloths (if any) clean; all table appointments—china, glass and cutlery—gleaming. Allocate to someone the task of attending to all cruets, sugar-sifters, sugar-bowls and sauce bottles (especially the necks). Make certain that ample supplies of cutlery, etc. are always available on the dumb-waiters for speedy resetting when required. Display tasteful menus that are legible and are not applicable to yesterday! Exercise constant care that all shaky tables and chairs and all worn sections of carpet (a positive danger) are repaired at once. Allocate seating accommodation fairly among all your waiting staff, allowing for popular and less popular tables. Install a system of general checking and control that will ensure that *every* item given out by the service-room is duly charged to and paid for by the patrons.

Have a restful *décor* and attractive lighting, enticing the public to enter and partake of refreshment.

Much of this may sound elementary, but all of it is of the utmost importance. The next time you visit a restaurant notice how many of these things are observed. You will be surprised how much has been neglected, even in some good-class places. No business is perfect. Always invite suggestions for improvements, both from your staff and from your patrons.

In a snack-bar or cafeteria, so much of the food is on display that it is imperative for presentation to be attractive. Endeavour to create an artistic sense in the staff of your kitchen and service-room, so that all dishes are so presented that they virtually sell themselves. Organize your staff so that at peak periods everyone is at action stations, thereby providing speedy service at the counter. Have some staff detailed to clear tables and empty ashtrays. It is extremely annoying for the patron when he has to dispose of his predecessor's used crocks before he can place his own tray of refreshment on the table.

Dress your front-line staff in well-cut, spotlessly clean overalls and caps. See that conditions generally are such that all members of the staff take a real pride in their appearance, and that this is reflected in the whole place. Avoid at all costs staff squabbles in the hearing of patrons. If your establishment is large enough to warrant it, consider offering prizes to those of the staff who attain a standard of excellence in some capacity. Apart from the material gain there is the pleasure derived from achievement.

Wherever the public may congregate, certain rules, regulations and directions are imperative. Nevertheless they should be confined to essentials, one of which is that relating to patrons' property. Here the wording varies considerably, according to the desire and attitude of the owners, but it is suggested that instead of the rather blunt " Proprietors do not accept liability " there should be used the more courteous " Proprietors may not accept liability ". While giving due protection this slightly indicates that, in the event of any genuine loss, the proprietors might make an *ex gratia* payment towards any financial loss. In some cases this intimation of non-liability is qualified by the words " unless patrons' property is deposited with one of the company's servants ".

" CASHIER " is preferable to " PAY HERE ".

Whether staff notices are necessary depends largely upon the size of the premises and the number of employees.

Fix definite hours of service and boldly display clear notices to that effect: in the case of a cafeteria from, say, 7.30 a.m. to 11 p.m.; in the case of a high-class restaurant, luncheons from 12 noon to 2.30 p.m., dinners from 6 p.m. to 11 p.m.

Much dissatisfaction can be caused by thoughtless or selfish patrons arriving for set meals too late to finish them before the establishment normally closes for the day. On these occasions attention should be tactfully drawn to this fact *before* the order is taken. It is not fair on the staff and, from the owner's point of view, it certainly does not pay to keep a few staff remaining late, plus lighting, for perhaps only two or three patrons.

Use tact when dealing with regular patrons on busy days such as local markets, race meetings, sporting events, etc. Never place them in the hands of your waiting staff; only supervisors should be given the duty of seeing to their comfort and service.

Christmas, Easter and other annual festivals, together with any local events of importance, should be suitably recognized.

ADDITIONAL SOURCES OF PROFIT

Many tea-rooms and restaurants find an additional source of profit in the manufacture and sale of pastries, pies, *hors d'œuvres*, cold sweets, etc. Effort should be made to keep this side of the business as distinct as possible from the catering side, so as to facilitate costing. Output should be sold to the selling section at cost, plus a determined percentage to cover overheads, they taking the profit made on the sale. Naturally the rate of profit on pastries, etc., made on the premises and consumed at the tables is higher than that on those bought and taken away by customers.

Most premises to-day carry stocks of cigarettes, book matches and block chocolate, which are a convenience to patrons and an additional source of profit to the establishment. It is usual for the cashier to attend to the stock and sale of these.

ADVERTISING

The best and cheapest form of real advertising is satisfied customers and patrons. Aim first of all at keeping your premises absolutely clean, attractively decorated and furnished; at providing china, glass and cutlery of a standard expected in the particular class of business; at preparing and serving food and beverages of a quality commensurate with the prices charged; at selecting staff who will enjoy working for and with you, and who will make patrons glad they came in. When you have attained this standard your advertising will be done for you by these patrons.

If you are a new owner do not make drastic changes too quickly, unless they are imperative. If they are abruptly introduced you may lose regular patrons, and new patrons are so often actuated by mere curiosity, which soon evaporates. Try to run the business a little better than the previous owner, making your changes and improvements gradually.

The small owner should act warily before spending money on advertising. He must first consider the location of his premises and the class of patron he wishes to attract. He must then choose such advertising media as will be seen by those potential patrons. If the premises are located in a city, his whole energy must be devoted to attracting workers from offices, warehouses, etc. Here advertising in the strictest sense is not vital, but in smaller towns, and in inland and seaside resorts where competition is keen and the season short, serious thought must be given to the question.

Whatever is attempted, never have anything cheap; the higher the class the better. The services offered by your establishment should be briefly described and well set out. Endeavour to hit on some point that will attract attention and bring you custom. As in most matters, it pays to consult the expert. When opening a new business or taking over a going concern, arrange in good time for the necessary publicity. Enlist the services of advertising agents and the local press. Much depends upon the type of establishment, but keep in mind general bill-posting and even the now somewhat old-fashioned sandwich-man.

" Displayed " advertisements in the local press are recommended; they usually yield much better results than small advertisements in the ordinary columns. To prevent loss of public interest insert your advertisement for a limited period, say three months, then give it a rest, either suspending it, or completely altering the lay-out, or inserting it in a competitive paper, should there happen to be one.

Other media are the local cinemas, rail and bus stations, the guide-books usually sponsored by and published under the auspices of local authorities, and hoardings. A large board on the roadside or in a convenient field a few hundred yards from your establishment will attract business.

Attention must be paid to the colour or colours used. Numerous persons are wholly or partially colour-blind. It has been discovered that women generally like pink, and men prefer blue. Many men cannot see red—that is, in colour! For posters, black lettering on a yellow background is effective.

The name of the establishment can have a distinct value. Try to get something original, while avoiding the bizarre and grotesque.

A permanent electric sign is a comparatively cheap form of advertising, and can be made available for twenty-four hours of each day.

Advertising applicable to hotels is discussed in the next chapter.

TRADE PUBLICATIONS AND THE CATERING EXHIBITION

Always subscribe to at least one trade publication, preferably two. The articles are always of interest, the recipes distinctly helpful, and the advertisements well worth perusal.

Some trade periodicals are:—

Caterer and Hotel Keeper, published weekly by the Practical Press Ltd., 1 Dorset Buildings, Salisbury Square, London, E.C.4.

Hotel and Catering Review, published monthly by the above.

Hotel Management and Restaurant Trade Journal, published monthly by Blandford Publications Ltd., 16 West Central Street, London, W.C.1.

Caterers' Journal, published monthly by Attwood & Co. Ltd., 7 Garrick Street, London, W.C.2.

Never miss the Catering Exhibition, which is held in January every second year at Olympia, London. The display of catering equipment is admirable, and a reminder that in this respect Britain is well to the fore. The show of artistically finished dishes is a real revelation of the art of chefs and *pâtissiers*, and the various demonstrations by catering students augur well for the future of the industry.

CHAPTER VIII

Hotel Administration—Reception Office—Bill Office—
Cash Office—General Accounts Department—House-
keeper's Department — Hotel Accounting — Visitors
Tabular Ledger—Cash Received Book and Sales (or
Sundry Debtors) Ledger—Cash Paid Book—Petty Cash
Book—Trading and Profit and Loss Accounts—Ordering
and Receiving Supplies—Control and Care of Food and
Stores—Control of General Stores—Control of Front of
the House—Control of Wines and Spirits—Hotel
Advertising

HOTEL ADMINISTRATION

FOR the general organization and management of a hotel
certain administrative departments are essential.

Reception Office

This is the intending guest's first point of contact with
the house. It should have readily available full and up-
to-the-minute information regarding every lettable room.
A board or chart on the wall should show at a glance: (a)
which rooms are let, to whom and at what rate, and possible
length of stay; (b) which rooms are vacant and available
for letting; and (c) which rooms are vacant, but not
available because of redecoration, etc. Before allocating
rooms for any period care must be taken that they will not
be required for guests who have booked in advance.

It is also the duty of the reception office to record all
departures. It should be in a position to give at any time
the exact number of guests occupying rooms, and the
number expected to arrive that day. Thus every movement
in and out must be carefully recorded, as well as all changes
by guests from one room to another. The reception office
must notify all movements to the bill office, the hall-porter
and the housekeeping department, as all these are actively
concerned.

Bill Office

This is an extremely important section, for it is responsible for the preparation of all accounts due to guests for the service that has been rendered. Here are collected and recorded the items to be charged, whether they be accommodation, a meal or a newspaper. It is not proposed at this juncture to enter into details of the system whereby checks are made out in duplicate by those rendering the service. Suffice it to say that one copy of each check must reach the bill office promptly, for it frequently happens that guests have to depart hurriedly and their bills have to be written up without delay.

Cash Office

Each bill presented with the requisite cheque or cash must be receipted in duplicate. In some establishments it is customary to paste on a slip authorizing the hall-porter to release the luggage belonging to the guest. The cash book kept in the cashiers' office is purely a receipt book, as it is unwise to allow payments of any nature to be made by a receiving cashier. Ordinarily there is a petty-cash float to meet small sundry outlays made on behalf of guests by the housekeeper and hall-porter.

In a number of hotels the reception office, the bill office and the cashiers' office are combined, the staff performing duties affecting each. Circumstances may render this necessary, yet it is not always satisfactory to have the same persons engaged on duties that should, strictly speaking, be entirely independent.

General Accounts Department

Its function is to collect, record and co-ordinate all the figures relating to every side of the business, so as to provide management with a complete picture in figures and percentages of the result of trading for any particular period of time.

Sometimes the control section is a part of this department, but in large establishments they are kept quite distinct. The choice of a control clerk, or a controller and his staff, is a matter demanding great care. The clerk or controller must be thoroughly versed in every detail of the business, and in him must be vested full authority to execute his duties, irrespective of whom it may involve. It is useless to expect efficient service from someone who is paid a low wage and is worked at top speed preparing schedules from numberless pieces of paper, many indecipherable. Those holding this onerous post must be accorded the status due to them.

Housekeeper's Department

This embraces a wide range of duties, and the choice of a housekeeper demands much care. Controlling a large proportion of the staff, usually female, she should be well versed in every branch of personnel management. Upon her rests also the responsibility for the care and condition of most of the house: bedrooms, bathrooms, toilets, corridors, stairways, staff quarters and all public rooms except the dining-room and the bars, the former being in the charge of the head waiter, the latter usually in the charge of the head barman.

All this involves the responsibility for carpets, curtains, furniture and bed linen, as well as the requisite stores for cleaning, etc. It is usual for the linen department, controlling the issue of clean and the reception of dirty linen and the necessary laundering and repairing, to be under the superintendence of the housekeeper.

HOTEL ACCOUNTING

This section should be read in conjunction with Chapter VI.

The basic books of record and account for hotels are:—

1. Visitors Tabular Ledger
2. Cash Received Book
3. Cash Paid Book
4. Petty Cash Book
5. Wages Book
6. Salaries Book
7. Staff Time Book
8. Purchase Day-book
9. Journal
10. Sales (or Sundry Debtors) Ledger
11. Purchase Ledger
12. General Ledger.

Some of these (i.e. 5, 6, 7, 8, 9, 11 and 12) have already been adequately dealt with in Chapter VI. In some establishments a sales day-book is used to record unpaid bills and accounts for banquets, hiring-out services and possibly outside catering. More often a sales day-book is rendered unnecessary by the use of the visitors tabular ledger.

The following notes cover the additional books of account required for a hotel as distinct from a cash-sales establishment.

Visitors Tabular Ledger

Any account not paid at the time of service—for example, a luncheon served in the restaurant or a visitor's bill—is transferred to this ledger direct, thus eliminating a sales day-book.

The basis of accurate charging to guests' accounts is by the issue of checks in duplicate by the section or department rendering the service.

It is a matter depending upon the desires of management, speed of service given to patrons, system of control in force and pressure of business, just how far the cashier or

Room No.	20	21	22	Restaurant	Café	Lounge
Name	Mr. Epps	J. Giddens	Mrs. Heath			
Brought forward	17 15 6	22 9 6	9 14 6	- - -	- - -	- - -
DEBITS						
Apartments	1 12 6	2 5 -	1 15 -	- - -	- - -	- - -
Breakfasts	3 6	5 6	4 6	- - -	2 19 6	- - -
Luncheons	7 6	1 10 -	- -	15 9 6	- - -	- - -
Teas	5 -		7 6	- - -	4 19 9	5 7 6
Dinners	1 5 6	1 14 -	8 6	21 2 9	- - -	- - -
Suppers	- -	- -	- -	5 4 6	17 2 3	- - -
Coffee	2 6	7 -	1 6	1 2 9	2 9 9	- - -
Wines	17 6	2 7 6	- -	7 15 6	- -	- - -
Spirits	- -	5 -	- -	1 2 9	- -	- -
Liqueurs	- -	7 6	- -	1 14 6	- -	- -
Beer	4 8	7 -	- -	1 9 8	- -	2 17 9
Minerals	1 6	2 6	1 6	12 4	- -	1 2 3
Cigars, Cigarettes	7 2	17 6	- -	2 4 9	- -	3 7 9
Telephone	- -	7 9	1 6	- -	- -	- -
Newspapers	6	1 2	9	- -	- -	- -
Laundry	- -	6 8	- -	- -	- -	- -
Car hire	- -	- -	- -	- -	- -	- -
Valeting	- -	7 6	- -	- -	- -	- -
Hairdressing	- -	- -	10 6	- -	- -	- -
Theatre tickets	- -	4 10 -	- -	- -	- -	- -
Sundries	3 3	- -	- -	- -	- -	- -
Paid out	- -	4 6	- -	- -	- -	- -
	£23 6 7	38 15 7	13 5 9	57 19 -	27 11 3	12 15 3
CREDITS						
Transferred to ledgers	- -	- -	- -	- -	- -	- -
Allowances	- -	- -	- -	- -	- -	- -
Cash received	- -	- -	- -	57 19 -	27 11 3	12 15 3
Balance carried forward	23 6 7	38 15 7	13 5 9	- -	- -	- -
	£23 6 7	38 15 7	13 5 9	57 19 -	27 11 3	12 15 3

TABULAR LEDGER "A"

Brasserie	Kiosk	Night Porter		Daily Total	Brought Forward	Carried Forward
– – –	– – –	– – –		49 19 6	871 16 10	921 16 4
			DEBITS			
– – –	– – –	– – –	Apartments .	5 12 6	45 10 –	51 2 6
– – –	– – –	– – –	Breakfasts .	3 13 –	7 19 –	11 12 –
4 3 6	– – –	– – –	Luncheons .	31 10 6	30 14 6	62 5 –
– – –	– – –	– – –	Teas .	10 19 9	2 – 6	13 – 3
7 14 9	– – –	– – –	Dinners .	42 5 6	41 17 9	84 3 3
5 19 9	– – –	– – –	Suppers .	28 6 6	19 4 6	47 11 –
1 3 9	– – –	– – –	Coffee .	5 7 3	3 1 9	8 9 –
7 3 9	– – –	– – –	Wines .	18 4 3	12 – 9	30 5 –
15 6	– – –	19 6	Spirits .	3 2 9	7 3 6	10 6 3
10 9	– – –	– – –	Liqueurs .	2 12 9	2 5 –	4 17 9
2 – 3	– – –	1 2 8	Beer .	8 2 –	9 16 –	17 18 –
14 –	– – –	2 3	Minerals .	2 16 4	4 7 6	7 3 10
			Cigars,			
2 5 6	3 7 9	1 – 4	Cigarettes .	13 10 9	5 19 6	19 10 3
– – –	– – –	– – –	Telephone .	9 3	3 1 9	3 11 –
– – –	2 4 3	– – –	Newspapers .	2 6 8	4 3 3	6 9 11
– – –	– – –	– – –	Laundry .	6 8	5 – 9	5 7 5
– – –	– – –	– – –	Car hire .	– – –	2 15 –	2 15 –
– – –	– – –	– – –	Valeting .	7 6	3 – –	3 7 6
– – –	– – –	– – –	Hairdressing .	10 6	2 7 6	2 18 –
– – –	3 7 6	– – –	Theatre tickets	7 17 6	10 2 6	18 – –
– – –	5 9	3 3	Sundries .	12 3	3 3 9	3 16 –
– – –	– – –	– – –	Paid out .	4 6	15 5	19 11
52 11 6	9 5 3	3 8 –		238 18 2	1098 7 –	1337 5 2
			CREDITS			
– – –	– – –	– – –	Transferred to ledgers	– – –	4 10 9	4 10 9
– – –	– – –	– – –	Allowances .	– – –	3 6	3 6
52 11 6	9 5 3	3 8 –	Cash received .	163 10 3	390 – 6	553 10 9
– – –	– – –	– – –	Balance carried forward .	75 7 11	703 12 3	779 – 2
52 11 6	9 5 3	3 8 –		238 18 2	1098 7 –	1337 5 2

Total business done for day £415 8 10

HOTEL VISITORS TABULAR LEDGER "B"

Room No.	Name	Apartments	Breakfasts	Luncheons	Teas	Dinners	Suppers	Coffee	Wines, etc.	Brought Forward	Total Debits	Cash	Allowances	Ledger Folio
	Brought forward								Columns for each heading as on "A"			and three additional cash columns for :— Transfer to ledger Total credits Carried forward		
20	Mr. Epps													
21	J. Giddens													
22	Mrs. Heath													
	Restaurant													
	Café													
	Lounge													
	Brasserie													
	Kiosk													
	Night Porter													

cash office can analyse the checks as they come in, and how much must be left to the control section later.

The control section should arrange for the collection of all cash checks and supply checks from cashiers, head waiters, kitchen, service-rooms, bars, etc. This should be done at the close of service of each meal and also where bars close at certain hours.

The visitors tabular ledger should incorporate all business done during each day. It corresponds to the daily summary prepared by the cashier in smaller establishments.

At the end of each week or month (usually month) the totals of the various columns should be analysed (if desired) and posted to the credit of the respective accounts in the general ledger, so as to provide sufficient information to the management of the volume of business done in each department. Often only one account is opened in the general ledger, this having the requisite number of columns.

In some hotels there is kept a monthly summary of the tabular ledger, which corresponds to the smaller establishment's summary book of goods sold. In it is recorded, analysed if desired, the day-to-day business done throughout the whole house. The totals are posted, usually monthly, to the general ledger, this taking the place of weekly or monthly postings from the tabular ledger.

Cash Received Book and Sales (or Sundry Debtors) Ledger

Whilst one cash book is sufficient for the small establishment, two distinct books are recommended for hotels: a cash received book, which is written up in the cash office, and a cash paid book (see below), which is written up in the accounts section.

The cash received book is a record of all cash (or cheques) received in payment of guests' bills, or from the restaurant or dining-rooms, lounges, bars, etc. It should include a column headed " Sundry Debtors ". When a guest leaves without settling his bill, the amount of it should be entered in the sundry debtors ledger, which is a separate book, being posted from the visitors tabular ledger (credit section), which is thereby correctly maintained. On the receipt of the guests' cheque in due course, the amount is entered in the cash received book and posted to the sundry debtors ledger.

The totals in the cash received book should be posted monthly to the *debit* side of a cash or bank account in the general ledger, thus forming a contra to the totals posted from the tabular ledger or monthly summary.

Cash Paid Book

In this are recorded all payments paid out in cash or by cheque and all amounts lodged in the bank. In the analysis columns are entered all such items of expense as are mentioned under **Cash Book** on page 89. If necessary there should be additional columns for interest, dividends, etc., paid, and capital expenditure on additional buildings, plant, equipment, etc.

All cheques drawn for wages, national insurance stamps and P.A.Y.E. should be entered in the cash paid book, and posted to the analysed columns on the debit side of the wages/salaries account in the general ledger.

Petty Cash Book

This is kept in the cash office. It should be columnar, the number of analysis columns being dependent upon the desires of management. One column should be for outlays made on behalf of guests, of which disbursements the bill office should be promptly notified, so that they can be added to the guests' bills. The petty cash book should be kept on the imprest system and dealt with in the same manner as suggested on page 90.

TRADING AND PROFIT AND LOSS ACCOUNTS

It is suggested that these are prepared more often than annually. Any extra work involved in preparing them half-yearly—or better still, quarterly—is so often amply repaid by the revelation of vital information that, if acted upon at once, prevents or reduces losses and may even increase present profit.

Despite all efforts there is always a time lag between the date of closing a financial period and the presentation of the final accounts for that particular period. This time lost is at least minimized by preparing accounts for shorter periods.

When the trial balance has been completed (see under **General Ledger,** page 93), the preparation of the trading account and the profit and loss account can be proceeded with. Before finalizing the various figures it is necessary to make certain provisions for expenses accrued and unpaid, and to take credit for those paid in advance and unexpired. Among these are wages and salaries, rent, rates, water, gas, electricity, interest, insurance premiums, business advertising, etc. In hotels intending guests may have paid deposits against future bookings. These sums should be separately treated, credited to a special account, and must appear as a liability. Provision must also be made for depreciation on the various assets, as well as for bad and doubtful debts.

At the interim balance, say six monthly, and at the end of the year the auditors should be asked to advise on any points of difficulty that may have arisen as to the form of the accounts, reserves for contingencies, and estimated liability for taxation.

In the catering industry stocks are, or should be, taken frequently, so little difficulty should be experienced with the trading account. It should show on the debit side:

(*a*) opening stocks of food, general stores (including cleaning materials), contents of wine cellars, bars, etc.; (*b*) amounts expended on purchase of new stocks during the period; and (*c*) gross profit. On the credit side should be shown total takings under headings: apartments, food, wines, etc.

The profit and loss account is in two sections. On the debit side of the first section should be shown: wages and national insurance, salaries and national insurance, rent, rates, fuel, gas and electricity, water, insurances, printing and stationery, advertising, general expenses, repairs, renewals, etc., and net profit. The credit side of the first section should show balance of gross profit. On the debit side of the second section should be shown depreciation written off such assets as buildings, plant and equipment, furniture, fixtures and fittings, motor vehicles, etc., the balance being the net profit subject to taxation and dividends (if any).

In preparing the trading and profit and loss accounts it is helpful for all concerned to show the figures for the corresponding period and extremely useful to show each expense heading as a percentage of the total turnover. In the case of a limited liability company the figures (to the nearest pound) for the previous year *must* be shown against each item set out in the profit and loss account and the balance sheet.

In addition to the foregoing all who are actively connected with *any* catering establishment should insist that weekly figures be prepared to show: (*a*) turnover under selected headings; (*b*) actual cost of all food consumed or used, after allowing for stocks at the start and finish of the period; (*c*) actual wages cost; (*d*) careful estimate of fuel, gas, electricity and water consumed; (*e*) equally careful estimate of every other overhead of the business; and (*f*) profit or loss during the period under review. Work out the percentages for each item.

It is advantageous to arrange these weekly statements in columnar form to facilitate comparison. Any material difference revealed should be immediately investigated. Figures representing business transactions over a period, if accurately compiled, can convey vital information and act as a guide for the future.

ORDERING AND RECEIVING SUPPLIES

With few exceptions no chefs or storemen should be given the power to order supplies. In the case of dry stores the storemen should prepare daily, and well in advance of possible needs, a note of items required. These should be checked by the control section against stocks held, and orders placed only with the authority of management. All orders should be in writing and, in larger establishments, made out in triplicate, the top copy going to the supplier, the second to the control section, the third remaining fast in the book.

More money is lost at the back door than many executives in the catering industry will admit. No one would dream of accepting nineteen shillings in exchange for a pound note, yet every day caterers accept short weight and inferior quality, to mention only two common sources of default.

Goods should be received and checked by a back-door porter, who might in some cases combine the duties of timekeeper. As far as possible *all* goods should be checked on arrival, whether food and drink or the numerous other articles that catering requires: furniture, china, glass, silverware, linen, stationery, general stores, etc. It is admitted that a large hamper of china will require to be signed for as " unexamined ", but none the less a strict check must be made of its contents on unpacking.

The back-door porter or whoever has the job of receiving goods should be furnished with two goods-received

E

(or goods-inwards) books or pads, which he should use alternately, sending to the control section each morning the book used on the previous day, which ensures a close check on all goods taken in. The fullest possible details of everything received should be recorded in the goods-received book, particularly: (a) date; (b) name of supplier; (c) quantity; and (d) description. There should be at hand a platform scale to check weights.

All perishable goods received should be sent direct to the kitchen or larder, other goods to the dry store, china and glass store, etc. The perforated top copy of the goods-received note is removed from the book and accompanies the relative consignment, the recipient signing the note and passing it on to the control section.

Storemen in the dry and other stores should be furnished with either books or numbered sheets for the recording of all receipts of stores. Perishables sent to the kitchen or larder should be fully recorded by the kitchen clerk or by whoever is deputed to carry out this work. Delivery notes should be attached to the sheets compiled daily by the storeman. Full credit for all goods, cases, cartons, etc., returned should be ensured by the institution of a returns or allowances book, in which all returns are recorded and duly signed for by the collector.

Suppliers should be instructed to send invoices direct to the accounts department.

CONTROL AND CARE OF FOOD AND STORES

Besides being fully capable the whole-time or part-time storeman or storewoman must be honest. The storeroom must be conveniently situated for both the receipt and issue of goods; it must be vermin-proof. It should be fitted with shelves, bins and cupboards, so that all stock can be stored in such a manner as to ensure rapid and efficient handling. The storekeeper should be provided with scales (balance and automatic), hammer, chisel, pliers, wire-cutter, cheese-cutter, scoops, brush and shovel.

Arrangement of all stock should be such that first in is first out. Tins, cases and packets can be placed on shelves or in cupboards, while flour, peas, beans, sago, sugar, etc., can be kept in large galvanized bins with fitted lids. Tea, being susceptible to odours and damp, should, as is usual, remain in the chests, which should be raised from four to six inches off the floor by bricks or blocks of wood, and placed clear of walls. See that the lids are kept on tightly and that chests are not in close proximity to soap or similar stores. In fact, if it is possible have a separate locked store for all cleaning materials and utensils.

A matter for decision is the hours during which the store shall be open. From 7.30 a.m. until 4 p.m. should be ample for all departments to obtain supplies, and allow time for the storeman to write up his records and tidy the store. Many chefs are guilty of ordering supplies just when they discover that they are short of the quantity immediately required. Instructions should be given to the chef —and to the storeman—that by, say, 4 p.m. anticipated requirements, both dry and perishable, for the following day's business should be made out on a requisition form of a large size.

No goods should leave any store without the production of a requisition note signed by some responsible person in the department concerned. All requisition notes should be in triplicate: two copies for the storeman, and one remaining fast. The recipient signs both copies as having received the goods and passes one to the control section, the storeman retaining the other for his own records. Careful note must be made of any alterations of quantities, and also where stores are out of stock.

The storeman should record all movements of his stock in a loose-leaf book—one page for each commodity, with which the name of the page should be headed. All initial stocks should be entered, followed by all receipts and issues. In columnar form should be recorded: (a) date; (b) all reference numbers of inwards and outwards chits; (c) name of supplier; (d) price and quantity. In a final column should be entered the stock remaining at the end of the week.

All stocks should be checked monthly with " spot " checks of various items from time to time. If possible this should be done by an independent person, who should be changed at intervals. While the quantities of stock are important, it is equally essential to note quality, general condition and rate of consumption of every item. Details of all stocktakings must be sent to the control section for pricing and extending, and due comparison with the figures shown in the storeman's stock register.

In large establishments there is usually one central store, from which a number of subsidiary stores are supplied. Whatever the number of stores may be, the same principles as set out above should be closely followed.

An adequate system of control over the kitchen operations is imperative, not only from the strictly business aspect, but also from the fact that morally such a check is essential in this particular type of enterprise. As the chef is supreme in his kitchen, the installation and operation of any system of control and costing should merit his acceptance. The best way of securing his active and whole-hearted support is to convince him that the system has been designed to prove clearly and accurately all the operations of his department. Should he also be paid a commission or bonus any opposition is usually swept away.

In passing it may be mentioned that often the need for effective control over the operations of any particular department can be measured by the " underground " opposition of the staff, whose favourite protest is that service will suffer and patrons complain!

Normally all perishables such as meat, fish, poultry,

vegetables and fruit pass direct to the kitchen from the goods entrance. In the main most of these are, or should be, used on the day of receipt or on the following day, stock left over being placed in the refrigerator or cold room. The chef should, of course, be provided with a storeroom or cupboard for all requisite dry stores.

If no kitchen clerk is available the chef should depute some responsible person to check all supplies coming in from the goods entrance and dry store. Items should be analysed under such collective headings as meat, poultry, fish, vegetables, fruit, groceries, tinned goods, milk, cream and fats. After allowing for opening and closing stocks, say weekly, the balance should represent cost of all supplies actually used. All incoming stocks having been debited to the kitchen, it is then credited with receipts for all meals served, and the difference should represent gross profit.

Work out the percentage and carefully compare it with previous results week by week. It is also informative to check apparent consumption of particular items against the menu in use and the number of meals served, as frequently the waiting and service-room staff have a taste for salmon, roast chicken, etc., for private consumption at a later moment. A detailed check on the larder often proves worth while, as does attention to all items sent up by the kitchen for the cold table in the dining-room or restaurant.

Here again stocks should be taken periodically by independent persons. A slight difficulty exists in this department as, unlike the general store, we have raw, partly cooked and fully cooked foods. In the main, take *all* stock and then price it out at cost, plus a proportion for wages, gas, electricity, solid fuel and other overheads incurred in preparing and cooking. Provided that the chef has a real business sense in addition to his cooking ability, the results should prove comparatively accurate.

CONTROL OF GENERAL STORES

These in the main are soaps, detergents, polishes, dusters, brushes of all descriptions, utensils such as pails and basins, toilet-rolls, electric lamps, greaseproof paper, drinking-straws, cocktail-sticks, etc. All are expendable, there being no actual cash return, so the cost of them is a direct charge against profits. Unless a strict check is kept on them it is amazing how much can be used and abused during a year.

Every precaution must be taken against waste and pilfering. Everything should be kept under lock and key, and given out only when required. Here again a loose-leaf record book should be kept on the same lines as suggested for the main store, no item being given out without the production of a signed requisition form. All articles needing replacement—worn-out brushes, burnt-out electric lamps, etc.—should be handed in to the store with the requisition form.

Monthly stocktakings are strongly recommended.

Strict attention must be paid to the control of stocks of china, glass, silverware, etc. Frequent inventories should be taken of the items held for daily use. Where more than one room is in use, take all stocks at one and the same time, to prevent stocks being rapidly moved to meet possible shortages in another room or section. Pilfering is common—and the staff are not always the guilty ones. Recently the following notice was seen: " Our cutlery is not like medicine, to be taken after meals."

Careful check must be made on all movements of linen. It is usual for the linen-room to issue clean against soiled returned. Signatures should be obtained for all linen issued to the various departments. All soiled linen must be closely examined for any damage due to accidents, or perhaps deliberately caused by some dissatisfied member of the staff. The time comes when linen ceases to be in a condition for issue for the use of guests and descends to the scale of usefulness to the staff and for other purposes. All such articles, which are known as discards, should be marked in such a manner as to identify them quickly. Coloured thread or tape is suggested, a distinctive colour being used for each year.

Trouble frequently arises in dealing with the laundry. Despite everything, " shorts " will happen and it is as well to institute a form of laundry register to keep track of all these recurring " shorts ". Check either that they are eventually produced by the laundry or that credit in some form is obtained towards replacement. Never allow this balance to go on for any length of time, as the job of sorting them out becomes a nightmare.

CONTROL OF FRONT OF THE HOUSE

It is essential that control be exercised on the activities of this department, such, for instance, as car hire and telephone services used by guests. Bookings for car hire are frequently made by the hall-porter and, if not paid for at the time, must be charged to the account of the guests concerned. The best plan here is to arrange for one reputable firm of car hirers to get all the business of the house at an agreed rate. Then all charges made by them can be checked against charges to be made against guests, on getting from them signed chits that they have actually had the service.

The telephone operator must record in a suitable form all calls made from the house. Twice a day this record should be collected by the control section, and the various charges made to guests on their accounts by the bill office. An analysis of the calls made will clearly show what is recoverable and whether the remaining calls are purely for the business of the house. Checking the accounts rendered by the Postmaster-General is sometimes laborious, but often repays.

CONTROL OF WINES AND SPIRITS

Owing to the high value of its contents the control of the wine-cellar should be absolutely strict. Many wine-cellars are badly planned, often inaccessible and do lend themselves to defalcations. No one other than actual cellar employees should ever be allowed in. Stock should be taken at frequent but irregular intervals by responsible and independent persons.

A stock ledger must be kept, recording opening stocks, additions, issues and closing stocks for each variety of wine, spirit, liqueur, etc. Orders should be placed only by management and after due consideration of present stocks, possible future requirements and, of course, the state of the market. The cellarman should record in triplicate full details of all supplies received, one copy for the accounts department, one for the control section, and the third remaining fast.

Issues of every description, whether for stock or replenishment, should be made only on receipt of numbered requisition notes signed by the managers of the selling departments, which may be of three kinds: (a) service or dispense; (b) cocktail; and (c) public. The requisition notes should be in triplicate, two going to the cellarman, the third remaining fast. The issue is signed for by the recipient on these two copies, which are left with the cellarman, who sends one to accounts and the other to control. If desired the cellarman can retain one copy to write up his stock ledger, thereafter passing it to control, but this is a matter of internal organization.

When circumstances permit, it is an excellent plan for control to collect all invoices, requisition notes, etc., covering all movements of cellar stock, and for the writing up of the stock ledger to be done in the control section.

Cellar stocktakings should be frequent and irregular. " Spot " checks of a few bins and shelves will keep the cellarman on his toes, he not knowing where and when the next check will be made. Watch must also be kept on cases, particularly those for beer and mineral water, as they are always charged. Wine cases are seldom charged and are usually sold at intervals, proceeds going, of course, to the credit of the hotel.

Stocktakings in bars should be daily, by independent persons changed from time to time. All barmen should be notified of the number of measures that each bottle of whisky, gin, liqueur, etc., must yield. Make periodical tests for possible adulteration. Occasionally stock may be lent by one bar to another, to meet sudden pressure of business. See that proper chits are exchanged for these. Institute a system of secret coding on all supplies from cellar to each particular bar, to guard against the bringing in of liquor from outside sources by staff anxious to keep their stock correct and to " make a bit on the side ".

Make sure that cash is received or checks made out for all liquor supplied. Checks should quote quantity, description or wine-list number, and price. After the conclusion of each period when the bars are open, the control section should collect all checks and chits for supplies issued and received. Cash should be cleared from the bars at the same time, and the cash-register recording-slip torn off. Fresh floats should be given for each period of opening, the bar manager being furnished by the cashier with a receipt for all such cash drawn.

Much more could be added to this section, but space does not permit. Possibly no other department requires such intensive and extensive checking, as opportunities for defalcation by smart-dealing barmen are numerous in many establishments.

The activities of the still-room also demand attention.

So often this department works more or less on its own, under the direct control of neither the housekeeper nor the chef.

HOTEL ADVERTISING

Wherever the hotel may be situated, travel guides—A.B.C., etc.—are the best sources of publicity. The last decade has seen such an enormous increase in travel, particularly by air and road, that carefully worded and nicely-set-out advertisements in these guides are almost certain to bring business.

Hotels situated in either inland or seaside resorts can avail themselves in addition of space in the local guide or town brochure, which usually has a most extensive circulation. Advertising in the national press is somewhat expensive and rather beyond the purse of the average hotelier. Exceptions are the many well-known hotels so favourably situated that a virtual fifty-two weeks' season is enjoyed. Again, many hotels de luxe have to keep their names constantly before their public by insertion of advertisements in the national press, including the better-class Sunday newspapers and the illustrated periodicals and magazines.

Many hoteliers at seaside resorts also find as excellent media the numerous weekly papers published in the busy industrial regions of the midlands and the north, west and east of England. These publications are widely read and are retained for some days, while the advertising life of the daily papers is naturally briefer.

Whatever media you choose, make absolutely certain that the contents of your insertion are truthful. Whether you possess a flair or not, it is wise to seek the advice of a reputable printer whose knowledge of style of type will be found distinctly helpful.

Beware of any caller who earnestly seeks to include your advertisement in the issue of some so-called guide or holiday brochure. These representatives are usually glib-tongued and so persistent that often fairly astute business men and women are hoodwinked into signing a contract and paying a deposit without carefully reading through the terms printed in the smallest possible type on the back of the agreement or contract. Many are those who have paid over cash they can ill afford for advertising schemes that either never reach fruition or appear in some practically unknown guide that may perhaps be displayed on counters of small shopkeepers or quiet station bookstalls. It is a sound maxim never to sign any contract or agreement before first reading over the proposed terms and conditions.

Hotel brochures deserve much greater thought than is sometimes given them. First set down on paper your thoughts and ideas, then submit them to your printer, who should be able to assist in style of type, general lay-out, and possibly get his artist or photographer to help. Again be absolutely truthful in all you say about your hotel and its services. Sketches or photographs should be equally relevant. Avoid making your brochure too wordy, confining it to the things that the majority of potential patrons will require to know.

1. Begin with a brief introduction setting out your offer of service, with any special inducements.

2. Give the exact location of the establishment. If it is at the seaside, state whether it is on the front. If it is not, be precise. Do not claim a view of the sea if it is visible only from the attic windows!

3. Quote your terms (inclusive if possible) per week, according to the season, position of room, and what services are included. Quote also your terms for children.

4. State extras such as morning tea, and coffee after meals.

5. State whether dogs are allowed and, if so, on what terms.

6. State whether a lift is available. This is an asset for elderly people. State also whether the premises are centrally heated.

7. State whether there are garage facilities.

8. Give brief particulars of local facilities for sport.

9. Include sketches (preferable to photographs) of the exterior of the premises, the lounge, the dining-room and one bedroom. Should there be a nice lawn or flower garden, show it as well.

CHAPTER IX

Composing Menus—Seasonal Foods—Fish, etc.—Vegetables—Game and Poultry—Hints on Serving—Some Common Kitchen Terms—Some Popular Garnishes and Accompaniments— The Wine-cellar — Wines — Spirits—Whisky—Gin—Rum—Brandy—Apéritifs— Liqueurs and Cordials—Other Beverages—Beer—Lager —Cider and Perry—Mead—Casks, Glass Containers, Measures—Some Definitions—Cigar Strengths

COMPOSING MENUS

IT is believed that the history of menus goes back to a banquet given in 1541 by a certain Duke of Regensberg. Apparently he had a lengthy piece of paper beside him, and one of his guests, being curious as to its contents, was informed that it was a list of dishes prepared by his chef or, as was more likely in those days, the Master of the Kitchen. This acted as a guide to the choice of available dishes.

In very many establishments it is an accepted custom that the chef writes out the menus, which may or may not be scrutinized by management. Strictly speaking, all menus should be *composed*, and it is the duty of management, in close consultation with the chef, to undertake this important duty. Some chefs, if left to themselves, will prepare menus comprising dishes that are easy to prepare and serve.

Composing a menu is not too simple a matter. Among the points to be observed are:—

1. The various dishes chosen must be such as are in season. Price paid is an important factor, as are the number of persons likely to be served, and their spending capacity.

2. The various dishes chosen for a complete luncheon or dinner menu must harmonize, varying in colour, taste, etc. For example: two white or two brown sauces

should never follow one on the other; no garnish or vegetable should appear twice; each dish should necessitate a distinct method of cooking.

3. Thought must be given to service requirements. When the menu has been finally decided upon, one copy should be retained by the chef, one by management, and a third sent to the printers or, if duplicated on the premises, to the typist.

All menus should be varied from day to day as far as is practicable. Give each course a title and make it sound attractive. One still sees:—

Soup
Roast Beef & 2 Veg
Sweet

How much more inducing to one's appetite is it to read something like:—

Cream of Fresh Tomato with Small Cracker Biscuits

———

Pan Fried Fillets of Dover Sole
Lemon Wedges

———

Roast Sirloin of Prime English Beef
Yorkshire Pudding
Rissolé and Parsley Potatoes   Braised Celery Hearts

———

Deep Dish Apple and Blackberry Pie
Ice-cream

———

Coffee

Set out your menus tastefully. Many establishments use menu cards supplied by well-known brewers, makers of soft drinks, etc. These are quite acceptable in restaurants, tea-rooms and cafés, but in hotels a plain folded card is to be preferred. On the front is the name of the hotel, the second, third and fourth sides being used for the menus of three meals: either breakfast, luncheon and dinner, or luncheon, dinner, and breakfast for the following morning. There is a distinct saving here, and guests can anticipate, we hope with pleasure, the next meal. An idea worth trying is to have the whole menu typed in small letters, with all the items beginning at the left-hand margin, and three spaces between the courses, thus:—

grapefruit cocktail

cream of tomato
consommé

fried fillet of plaice—tartare sauce
grilled cod steak—butter sauce

roast lamb—mint sauce—fresh peas—new potatoes
fried liver and bacon—sauté potatoes
home-boiled ham and tongue—salad

jam sponge and custard sauce
compote of fruit
ices—vanilla and strawberry

biscuits, butter and cheese

coffee

Short menus help variation. Try to introduce a fresh dish once or twice a week, especially if you have a number of regular patrons. Cultivate the co-operation of your chef and head waiter in getting away from the usual mashed or creamed potatoes. Offer plain boiled, roast, chipped, or fried with onions, which is known as *lyonnaise*. Milk puddings can be much more appetizing if baked, and served with fruit.

Breakfast menus are often dull and most uninteresting. On arrival at a large, gloomy terminus in a city after a long journey by night, it adds to one's feelings of depression to be presented with a breakfast menu that is a replica of dozens of others all over the country. It so often happens that toast is cold and leathery, coffee and tea weak and just warm, porridge stodgy, and bacon either raw or burnt. No wonder many travellers derive more pleasure from a persual of the morning paper.

The following is a suggestion of what could be offered to your patrons:—

Grapefruit Suprême
Cereals
Scotch Porridge with Fresh Cream
A Selection of Chilled Fruit Juices—Tomato, Pineapple,
Orange or Grapefruit

———

Grilled Royal Kippers
Poached Haddock
Composite Dishes to Choice—
Egg   Bacon   Tomato   Mushrooms
Sauté Potatoes   Chipolatas

———

Rolls   Croissants
Toast   Marmalade
Honey

———

Tea or Coffee

From time to time correspondence appears in our national press on the subject of menus being written in French. Strictly speaking, dishes that are French in origin must be shown in the French language, while real English dishes should be in English. Welsh Rarebit would look as ridiculous in French as would *Sole Duglère* in English. If a dish is given a name known internationally it should be served according to the accepted recipe.

Give thought to *table d'hôte* or *à la carte* menus. The first economizes in service, reduces the number of dishes to be prepared and enables the kitchen staff to concentrate. Its adoption, however, often alienates the patron who likes to choose his dishes from a comprehensive menu. Experience has proved that *à la carte* is the better of the two.

Goodwill can be created by making a feature of one

particular dish. No matter whether it be steak-and-kidney pudding or jam roll, endeavour to excel in its preparation and service.

Remember to provide at least one vegetarian dish each day. They are always appreciated, often by others than strict vegetarians.

Many establishments make a feature of their wine list, but a well-produced soft-drink list can secure additional trade.

Where space permits set up a table in your dining-room for a display of cold meats, salads and cold sweets. If this is close to the entrance it may well prove a source of interest to your patrons and profit to yourself.

SEASONAL FOODS

The following are given only as a guide. The rapid advances made in recent years in the preservation of foods of all kinds by refrigeration, deep freezing, etc., have made it possible for caterers to purchase a large proportion of the undernoted, particularly vegetables, all the year round. Experience will probably prove that of all vegetables, green peas are the best when frozen, and certainly the most popular with all your patrons.

Large sums are being spent on research in order to devise and perfect means and methods not only of preserving food for long periods, but also of satisfactorily retaining natural flavours.

Fish, etc.

Cod	.	.	.	. July to April
Halibut	.	.	.	. May to January
Lobster	.	.	.	. June to September
Mussels	.	.	.	. September to April
Oysters	.	.	.	. September to April
Plaice	.	.	.	. May to January

Salmon	.	.	.	.	February to September
Smelt	.	.	.	.	October to May
Sole	.	.	.	.	June to February
Trout	.	.	.	.	March to September
Turbot	.	.	.	.	July to May
Whitebait	.	.	.	February to August
Whiting	.	.	.	.	August to May

Vegetables

Artichoke, Globe	.	.	November to June
Asparagus	.	.	.	March to August
Beans, Broad	.	.	June to August
Beans, French	.	.	June to September
Beetroot	.	.	.	August to March
Cauliflower	.	.	.	July to December
Celery	.	.	.	.	August to March
Parsnips	.	.	.	November to March
Sea-kale	.	.	.	December to May
Spinach	.	.	.	.	All year
Sprouts, Brussels	.	.	October to January

Game and Poultry

Game, Black	.	.	.	August to December
Grouse	.	.	.	.	August to December
Guinea Fowl	.	.	Spring months
Hare	.	.	.	.	August to February
Partridge	.	.	.	September to February
—— Eggs	.	.	.	October to March
Pheasant	.	.	.	October to January
Plover	.	.	.	.	October to March
—— Eggs	.	.	.	April
Quail	.	.	.	.	October to February
Snipe	.	.	.	.	October to March
Teal	.	.	.	.	October to February
Turkey	.	.	.	.	December to January
Woodcock	.	.	.	August to March

HINTS ON SERVING

Beef and ham should be cut very thin; lamb, mutton, pork and veal thicker. Roast turkey, goose and roast duck are generally served stuffed, and a spoonful of stuffing is served on each plate.

Young game birds—e.g. grouse, partridge and pigeon— are served whole. The larger, older birds are split into two portions. Pheasant is carved in thin slices. Skilful carving means dainty presentation, the appearance of full portions, and economy in consumption.

Toast Melba is served on a folded serviette covering the plate.

Caviare is the specially treated roe of the sturgeon.

Foie gras is made from the liver of the goose.

Oysters should be served with cut brown bread and butter, lemon wedges and cruet.

A chafing-lamp, in which methylated spirit is used, is placed on a service trolley for heating up, if required, dishes before actual service at the table; and for making omelets and special pancakes, e.g. *crêpes suzette*.

Table-napkins are now universally recognized as an essential in all good-class restaurants and hotels. The practice of folding is not now general; custom dictates that minimum handling is preferable.

SOME COMMON KITCHEN TERMS

A la broche.—Roasted on a spit in front of the fire.

À la carte.—Dish on the menu, with set price and cooked to order.

Au four.—Baked in an oven.

Au gratin.—Cooking completed under a grill or sala-mander.

Bain-marie.—Piece of kitchen equipment, often on top

of hot closet, comprising a metal bath filled with hot water in which are placed saucepans, etc., to keep contents hot without burning.

Béchamel.—One of the kitchen's basic sauces (white).

Bordelaise.—Rich, brown sauce flavoured with wine.

Bouchée.—Small patty.

Canapé.—Small, shaped piece of fried or toasted bread, on which are placed savouries or *hors d'œuvres*.

Casserole.—Earthenware or copper stewpan.

Crêpe suzette.—Pancake having a specially prepared sauce and "flamed" with brandy in the sight of the patron.

Entremets.—Hot or cold sweet.

Flambée.—Dish finally prepared and "flamed" with a liqueur in the sight of the patron.

Fricassee.—Brown or white stew of veal or chicken.

Jambon.—Ham.

Poule.—Fowl.

Poulet.—Chicken.

Poussin.—Young chicken.

Ragoût.—Very rich, brown stew.

Ris de veau.—Sweetbread.

Sauce Suprême.—Sauce made with chicken stock, cream, mushrooms, lemon, white wine, etc.

Sauerkraut.—Pickled white cabbage.

Tournedos.—Circular fillet of beef, about three-quarters of an inch thick.

Vol-au-vent.—Light puff-pastry case for filling with minced chicken, etc.

SOME POPULAR GARNISHES AND ACCOMPANIMENTS

Roast beef.—Horseradish sauce, Yorkshire pudding.

Roast chicken.—Bread sauce, game chips and rich gravy.

Roast duck.—Apple sauce and green peas.

Roast goose.—Apple sauce and green peas.

Roast lamb.—Red-currant jelly or mint sauce.

Roast mutton.—Onion sauce.

Roast turkey.—Cranberry sauce.

Boiled fowl.—Parsley sauce or boiled rice and *sauce suprême*.

Stewed lamb.—Green peas and caper sauce.

Game in general.—Bread sauce, toasted bread-crumbs, game chips and rich gravy.

Jugged hare.—Red-currant jelly.

Salmon (hot).—Hollandaise sauce and cucumber.

Salmon (cold).—Mayonnaise sauce, cucumber, lettuce-and-tomato salad.

THE WINE-CELLAR

Unless you already possess detailed knowledge of the wine and spirit trade, it is wise to place yourself in the hands of a reputable wine-merchant, who will guide you as to what to purchase and when to do so. Should your establishment be small he will take stock at appointed dates and replenish your bins, etc. With a larger establishment the cellar, bars, etc., must be staffed with the best employees procurable.

Wine-cellars should be underground, dry, free from draughts, with tiled or concrete floors, adequately lighted, absolutely clean, of an average temperature of 54° F., regularly fumigated to destroy pests, and lime-washed annually. According to requirements they should be divided into storage for casks and binning sections for wines and spirits.

Equipment should consist of binning compartments, scantling, cullet bins,[1] spare casks, filter, and a machine for corking, capsuling and labelling, which last operation can be performed by hand. Bottle-washing is preferably done elsewhere than in the cellar. Items of small equip-

---

[1] For this and other terms see glossary, pages 159–161.

ment are: thermometer, dip-rod, pails, bowls and taps, brace and bit, rouser, slogger, Sykes's hydrometer, racking hose, valinch, testing-glass, book of reducing tables, finings- and tasting-glasses.

Each wine-bin should be allocated a permanent number corresponding to that on the wine-list. To avoid errors and save time all orders by wine butlers are for " 1 bottle of No. 73 " instead of " 1 bottle of Liebfraumilch ". To keep the corks wet and prevent shrinkage, all wines should be stored on their sides in their respective bins—one row having the corks facing outwards, the succeeding row the reverse, and so on according to the quantity. To facilitate stocktaking all labels should be clearly visible. Old ports should have two white lines smeared along the length of each bottle, to indicate how it should be placed without disturbing the liquor.

Champagne and other sparkling wines must also be binned on their sides; the least shrinkage of a cork will allow the gas to escape, rendering the wine flat and tasteless. Spirits, on which cork has a different effect, must be stored upright.

Beer and cider, whether in cask or bottle, should be stored in the cellar and kept at an even temperature. All deliveries should be sold in strict rotation, to avoid risk of deterioration.

WINES

The Wine and Spirit Association of Great Britain has adopted the following definition:—

"Wine is the alcoholic beverage obtained from the fermentation of the juice of freshly gathered grapes, the fermentation of which has been carried through in the district of its origin, and according to local tradition and practice."

The principal wine-producing countries of the world are France, Italy, Germany, Spain, Portugal, Greece, Austria, Hungary, Luxembourg, Madeira and Algeria.

In addition there are British and Empire wines. Australia produces many fine ones. The best South African wines come from the Paarl and Stellenbosch areas. Cyprus also sends out her quota. British-made wines, chiefly of the port and sherry types and vermouths, are generally of good quality.

The juice resulting from the first pressing of the grapes is called must. This ferments of its own accord, due to the fact that the bloom on grapes is natural yeast fungus. After the first fermentation the deposit sinks to the bottom of the cask. The wine is then drawn off into fresh casks, in which a second fermentation takes place. When fermentation is complete the liquor is racked—that is, transferred from one cask to another. This may have to be done more than once before the full maturity required for bottling is attained.

Wine may be blended or unblended, the latter being the produce of the grapes grown in one particular vineyard in one year. Blended wines are more usual. Sparkling (or " made ") wines have a liqueur of brandy and sugar added. They are bottled *before* the second fermentation, thus retaining the carbonic acid gas that produces the effervescence. Natural wines are those that are allowed to ferment fully, the result being a dry or a sweet wine according to the sugar content of the grapes. As fermentation ceases after a certain proportion of alcohol is produced, sugar may still remain unconverted into alcohol, giving a sweet wine. In some cases brandy is added in the early stages of fermentation, checking further action; these are known as fortified wines. White wines can be made from either black or white grapes, red wines from black grapes only. *Rosé* or pink wines can be produced from the vinification of black grapes, but the skins are excluded from the must prior to the fermentation. Other methods are by mixing black and white grapes, blending red and white wines, and even by addition of colouring matter.

Correct service of wine is important. All glasses in general should have stems and be made of clear, plain, thin glass. Their shape should vary according to the wine: for a sparkling wine, a tulip-shaped glass with a star cut in the bottom; for sherry, a long, thin glass; for port, an egg-shaped glass; and for brandy, the fairly large bowl-shaped type known to the French as *ballon*.

All glasses should be carefully washed and dried with cloths kept for the purpose. When unpacking new stocks always thoroughly wash after removing the thin packing paper, which can impart an undesirable taste.

Wines appropriate to the various courses are:—

Hors d'œuvres . . .	Sherry, French or Italian vermouth or cocktails
Soup	Dry sherry or Marsala
Fish	Still hock or Sauterne
Entrée	Red claret or a light red Burgundy
Relevé or joint . .	Red Burgundy or Chianti
Game	Champagne or red Burgundy
Entremets . . .	Champagne or Sauterne
Dessert—cheese or fruit .	Port or brown sherry
Coffee	Liqueurs

Sparkling wines (champagne, etc.) and white wines should be served chilled, while all red wines should be served at room temperature.

SPIRITS

The best known are whisky, gin, rum and brandy. They are the distilled products of fermented liquors, whisky and gin being derived from malted and unmalted grains, rum from molasses, and brandy from the juice of grapes.

Whisky

The world's finest is produced in Scotland, where a combination of excellent grains, soft water, drying of the grain by peat, and an enviably high standard of skill derived from many years of experience produce an unrivalled whisky.

The fermented grain may either be malted or unmalted, the former being known as a malt whisky and produced in a pot still; the latter being known as grain whisky and being produced in a patent still. Barley is used exclusively for malt whisky; barley, oats and maize for grain whisky.

Most of the distilleries are situated in the Scottish highlands. Half are in the counties of Banff, Moray and Nairn, where are situated the world-famous malts of Strathspey, Speyside and Glenlivet. Most whiskies now sold are blended, i.e. a mixture of the products of pot stills of different ages, but of the same distillery. The art of blending is highly technical, much care and thought being exercised to attain the correct proportions and, by combination of the characteristics of the various products, to achieve a perfect and harmonious whole.

Whisky cannot be sold until it is three years old, but the best blends are usually seven or more years of age before they are released. The amber colour is obtained from the casks in which the whisky is left to mature. These are usually sherry casks, which are ideal for this purpose. Caramel is sometimes added for colouring.

Ireland also contributes to the world supply. Owing to the difference in the water and peat used, and to the fact that it is produced in *one* operation from a mash of matter and unmalted grain in a pot still, Irish whiskey— spelt with an " e "—is quite distinct in flavour from the Scotch. Taking longer to mature it is usually at least seven years old before it is sold.

Of American whisky there are two varieties. Rye, as its name implies, is made from rye; Bourbon from maize.

Gin

This spirit was originally made in Holland by a doctor as a medicine against attacks of scurvy and similar troubles contracted by seamen in the Dutch sailing-vessels of olden days on their long voyages to the Far East. It was called

F

genièvre, this being the French for juniper. From this came the Dutch *jenever* and the English geneva, which became shortened to gin.

It is distilled in a patent still and then rectified, the grain used being unmalted maize. Sometimes it is made from imported molasses spirit. Flavouring matters are numerous, each maker having his own secret recipe. Juniper is predominant, but there are many others, such as coriander and angelica.

The rectified spirit does not improve with age, so, after the few weeks required to blend spirit and flavourings, it is ready for sale.

Rum

Rum is a by-product in the manufacture of cane-sugar. The principal centres of production are Jamaica (British West Indies) and Demerara (British Guiana), but it is also produced in other parts of the West Indies, Cuba, Mauritius, Natal, and in Dutch Guiana.

The distillation of the wash, derived from various processes to which the original cane has been subjected, is done in a pot still, fermentation taking three days. What is known as vapour from a charge (1,500 gallons) of wash passes into two retorts (known as low wine and high wine), but only the real heart of the distillation, approximately seven per cent, becomes actual rum. The quantities of low wine and high wine remaining are returned to their respective retorts. The actual spirit is now white, and is coloured with caramel to meet the desires of consumers.

A period of three years in cask for maturity is required before the spirit can be sold in Britain. As with all spirits, there are numerous blends and flavours to satisfy the varying demands.

Brandy

Sometimes called the King of Spirits, it is distilled from wine. France is pre-eminently the producer of the world's finest brandies, the region of Cognac and Armagnac being specially famous. Brandies of excellent quality are also obtained from Spain, Portugal, Australia, South Africa and Cyprus.

Age is an important factor in brandy. The longer it is kept in cask the finer becomes the bouquet, the richer the colour and, although the alcoholic content is reduced, the higher the medicinal value. Although the strength is lower than at first, it is still, even after some years, higher than is normally consumed. A limit—normally forty to seventy years—is set for its retention in cask. When bottled it remains static.

Identifying markings are :—

Brandy		Cognac	
V.O.	Over 5 years	V.O.	Over 10 years
V.S.O.P.	Over 10 years	V.S.O.P.	Over 25 years
X.O.	Over 40 years		

APÉRITIFS

Apéritifs are beverages used as appetizers. Sherry is probably the most consumed. Next comes vermouth. White wines and numerous flavourings are used in the French variety, brandy being added to give additional strength. Italian vermouth is usually darker and sweeter, due to the basic wines used. British vermouths are excellent.

For the flavouring of drinks various bitters are manufactured, the most famous being angostura, which is made in the West Indies. Other bitters are apricot, peach, Fernet Branca and Campari. They must always be used sparingly.

Cocktails, which have become so popular during the last two decades, are mixtures of wine and/or spirits along with such other ingredients as fruit juices, all in varying proportions. Each cocktail has a distinctive name, and a list would cover pages of this book.

LIQUEURS AND CORDIALS

These beverages are extremely popular as a final touch to an excellent dinner, being usually accompanied by black coffee. Generally liqueurs can be defined as alcoholic beverages, sweetened and flavoured by either the infusion or distillation of aromatics and/or fruit substances along with potable spirit. All components must be meticulously dissolved and mixed. Many of the recipes are secret and have been handed down for centuries.

Two famous liqueurs are Benedictine and Chartreuse. The first was originally made by the monks of Fécamp in Normandy, the second by the monks of La Grande Chartreuse Monastery, Grenoble.

The following list gives some liqueurs and their flavours:—

Absinthe	.	Aniseed
Advocaat	.	Brandy and yolk of egg
Anisette	.	Aniseed
Benedictine	.	Angelica and aromatic herbs
Chartreuse	.	Angelica and aromatic herbs
Cherry Brandy	.	Cherry
Cointreau	.	Orange, very dry
Crème de Cacao	.	Cocoa and vanilla
Crème de Menthe	.	Peppermint
Crème de Noyan	.	Bruised almonds
Curaçao	.	Orange
Drambuie	.	Scotch whisky and heather honey
Grand Marnier	.	Orange
Kirsch	.	Cherry
Kummel	.	Caraway-seed
Maraschino	.	Cherry
Milk Punch	.	Rum, milk and spices
Peach Brandy	.	Peach

Cordials are similar in some respects to liqueurs, some of them having been designated as such. They are produced by the steeping, maceration or mixing of aromatics and/or fruit substances with potable spirit, in a manner and method similar to the making of liqueurs.

OTHER BEVERAGES

Beer

Though called the Englishman's drink, this is a most valuable export. It is brewed in districts where the water is suitable, particularly in the London area, Burton-on-Trent and Edinburgh. The main constituents are malted barley and hops. After being germinated by steeping in water, the sprouting being arrested by kiln drying, the barley is crushed, mashed with hot water, then boiled with the hops. When cooled the wort is fermented by adding yeast.

Lager

Made now in Britain, its original home was the Continent, principally Denmark and Germany. The method of brewing varies somewhat from that for beer, a yeast that works at a lower temperature being used. To mature it and develop the required flavour, lager is usually stored for six months at a low temperature.

Cider and Perry

These are made from the fermented juice of apples and pears respectively. The demand for cider is considerable, but perry is produced in much smaller quantities. Cider production is mainly in the western counties of England—Worcester, Gloucester, Hereford, Somerset and Devon—but it is also produced in Kent, Norfolk and Suffolk. Sweet and dry varieties are made.

Cider and perry bear a lower rate of duty than wines and beers, but a licence similar to that for beer is required for their sale.

Mead

It is similar to a light wine, but is made from the fermentation of honey, the flavour being derived from the flowers that give the honey. Briefly the art depends upon correct fermentation, addition of a certain quantity of water at the correct temperature, and the carrying out of the process in darkness. In origin Anglo-Saxon, its manufacture has been energetically revived at Gulval in Cornwall and at Princes Risborough in Bucks.

CASKS, GLASS CONTAINERS, MEASURES

Casks

Beer	B.I.G.[1]		Whisky[2]	B.I.G.
Pin	4½	Octave		18
Firkin	9	Quarter Cask		28
Kilderkin	18	Hogshead		55
Barrel	36			
Hogshead	54			

Wines and Spirits	B.I.G.
Pipe.—Lisbon	117
Port and Tarragona	115
Marsala	93
Madeira	92
Puncheon.—Brandy	120
Rum	93–114
Hogshead.—Wine	63
Tun.—Wine (4 hogsheads)	252

Glass Containers

	Fluid Ozs.	To B.I.G.
Standard Bottle	26⅔	6
„ Half Bottle	13⅓	12
Imperial Quart	40	4
„ Pint	20	8
„ Half Pint	10	16
Reputed Quart (Standard Bottle)	26⅔	6
„ Pint (Standard Half Bottle)	13⅓	12

Magnum.—Bottle containing two reputed quarts.
Jeroboam.—Double magnum.
Rheoboam.—Capacity of six brandy bottles (rare).

---

[1] British imperial gallon, 160 fluid ounces.
[2] These casks are made from good oak only. Sherry casks are widely used.

Measures

Gill or Quartern.—Quarter of a pint, equal to 5 liquid ounces. The standard bottle contains $5\frac{1}{3}$ gills or quarterns.

Nip or Noggin.—One-sixth of a gill or quartern.

Optic.—A " five-out " optic gives one-fifth of a gill or quartern, i.e. 26 per bottle. A " six-out " optic gives one-sixth of a gill or quartern, i.e. 32 per bottle.

SOME DEFINITIONS

Aerometer.—Instrument used for measuring specific gravity.

Beeswing.—Floating crust of a light nature sometimes found in port. It resembles an insect's wing and is quite harmless.

Bodega.—Spanish word for warehouse where wine is stored.

Bouquet.—Perfume of wine.

Brut (French).—Very dry (of champagne).

Cradle.—Wicker basket used for serving red wines which must be kept in a horizontal position and served with care.

Crust.—Deposit in old bottled wines.

Cullet bin.—Usually for broken glass.

Decant.—To transfer wine from one bottle to another or to a decanter. This is done to avoid deposit.

Demijohn.—Glass vessel holding from three to ten gallons. It is of a bulging shape, narrow-necked and usually wickered.

Demi-sec.—Half dry.

Fine Maison.—French term for liqueur brandy of the house or hotel.

Finings.—Material for clarifying wines, etc.

Mash.—Crushed malt, etc., steeped and stirred in hot water to form wort.

Must.—New wine; grape-juice before fermentation is complete.

Optic.—Instrument for dispensing exact measures of whisky, etc.

Patent Still.—Continuous still producing neutral spirit with a rectifying action.

Pot Still.—A single-action still for producing malt whisky.

Potheen.—Irish whiskey illicitly distilled.

Punt.—Refers to the pushed-in end of a bottle, done to add strength.

Racking.—Drawing off wine from the lees in one cask and transferring it to another cask.

Rouser.—Instrument for stirring boiling wort.

Slogger.—Heavy wooden mallet.

Sorbet.—Water ice flavoured with a liqueur.

Stillion.—Stand for a cask of beer or wine.

Sweets.—Term used by Customs and Excise Department for British wines and cordials.

Tierce.—Roughly one-third of a pipe or cask, equalling 35–40 gallons.

Ullaged.—Term applied to a bottle or cask when part of the contents has evaporated, leaked or been otherwise withdrawn.

Underproof.—Containing less alcohol than proof spirit.

Valinch.—Large glass tube used for taking samples from casks.

Vintage.—Term applied to wines of a particular year and from a definite estate, e.g. Champagne, Burgundy, Hock, etc. Sometimes the addition of a vintage date does not indicate a wine of really exceptional quality, but merely that of a good year.

Wash.—Fermented wort from which spirit is distilled.

Weepers.—Binned wine bottles that are leaking at the

corks. The wine must be either immediately consumed or rebottled, for deterioration is rapid.

Wort.—Infusion of malt before it is fermented into beer.

CIGAR STRENGTHS

Claro.—Mild.	Colorado.—Strong.
Colorado Claro.—Medium.	Maduro.—Strongest.

CHAPTER X

CATERING FOR FUNCTIONS

CATERING for formal functions and social gatherings is one of the most important branches of the industry. In the planning of this service thought must be given to the various requirements of the different classes involved, from a civic banquet to a private cocktail party. First of all make quite certain that you have adequate facilities in the way of accommodation and equipment, satisfying yourself that you have ample furniture, linen, china, glass and cutlery to meet every need without drawing on supplies required for daily business. Never allow functions of any kind whatever to interfere with that. Make certain too that your kitchen and service-rooms are equal to the demands that may be made on them. Consult your chef and your head waiter or manageress as the case may be.

Having gauged local requirements, assessing as far as possible the number and variety of functions for which you may be called upon to cater, and having decided which types can be successfully undertaken with the accommodation and equipment at your disposal, you are in a position to proceed.

Advertising can be most expensive and futile. Only by the exercise of every care can adequate results be achieved. It is usually worth while to prepare a brochure, setting out the fullest information relating to the various functions you can undertake, and giving specimen menus, estimates of costs, and a few really good photographs of your suites.

All inquiries should receive prompt and courteous attention. Arrange for some suitable member of the staff to act as receptionist to all callers and to attend to inquiries by post and telephone. Every care must be taken of all correspondence relating to booked functions. Use a foolscap diary—one page for each day—and record therein under the appropriate date the following details: (a) full name and address of the person, association, etc., booking; (b) expected numbers; (c) hours of commencing and finishing; (d) menu chosen (in full); (e) time of service; (f) price per head, and whether inclusive or not; (g) any special requirements such as band or orchestra; services of toastmaster or photographer; cakes, etc., for wedding parties; hire of piano; playing cards and scoring cards for whist and bridge parties; and so on.

COSTING AND CONTROL

Where a banquet trade of any magnitude is conducted it is wise to segregate costs as far as possible from those of the everyday business of the establishment. It is usual to have a banqueting manager, with perhaps an assistant, a secretary/typist to attend to correspondence and telephone calls, and a few reliable permanent waiters. Casual waiters can be engaged as required. The majority of banquets being booked well ahead of the due dates, it is possible to make forward plans.

Supplies of linen, glass, cutlery, etc., should be self-contained. Losses are fairly high in this department, so the taking of almost daily inventories is well-nigh imperative. Where the volume of trade warrants it, it is advisable to place a member of the staff in full charge of these valuable accessories.

The following are the main items that must be included

in your costings: (*a*) charge for use of suite, which should include wear and tear of furniture, carpets, fittings, etc.; (*b*) heating and lighting; (*c*) use and wear and tear of all china, glass, cutlery and linen; (*d*) laundry charges for linen used; (*e*) flowers and other decorations; (*f*) cost of all food and its preparation; (*g*) wages of all staff involved, either directly or indirectly—supervisors, chef, kitchen and service-room staffs, waiters and waitresses, barmen, porters and other attendants. Keep in mind the cost of staff meals and the possibility of overtime. Wines are usually charged on the basis of consumption. Remember to include wages of wine butlers and wine waiters, and to charge corkage should the party supply its own wines.

You may be asked to provide the cake for a wedding reception and to post pieces of it to absent friends. The charge for the cake should include the cost of all bags and boxes, packing and postage. Again, charge must be made for all confetti, rose leaves, streamers, balloons and all the other nonsense that custom demands must mark the going away of the couple.

Where you are asked to provide a dance band or orchestra this must also be charged, along with any meals or other refreshment supplied to the musicians. A hire fee for the piano is usual, as is the payment of commission to the caterer by the dance bands, orchestras and photographer for introductions that lead to bookings.

It is wise to revise costing figures from time to time. In fact, prepare a costing statement for every function, in order to satisfy yourself that your charges are really covering all costs and leaving you a reasonable margin of profit. Admittedly efficient carrying through of functions is a comparatively cheap form of publicity, but in view of the planning and work involved, adequate financial return must be secured.

In the service of wine very strict measures must be taken to guard against defalcation, theft, etc. The value is high and the temptation great. When dinner tickets include cocktails, here is a potent source of danger. By strict check it is possible to know the actual consumption of, say, sherry, but as cocktails involve a variety of liquors such check is not conclusive. While the majority of guests may content themselves with one cocktail, others will have four or five if they get the opportunity. Where cash is paid for each drink served, the position is better and a closer control can be attained.

The various bars and dispense for this department are supplied direct from the cellar. Initial orders and all replenishments from time to time must be issued only on requisition notes signed by such responsible persons as the banqueting manager or his assistant. Chits should be in triplicate (see page 136). For all these supplies the cellar receives credit and the banqueting department is debited.

No wine, etc., should ever be served from any bar or dispense without a chit from the waiter. This should show the description of the wine, or the bin number, and the price charged. All wine waiters receive a float and, before going off duty, must account for this sum and for all supplies received or bought from the bar or dispense. To cope with this side it is necessary to have clerical staff, well versed in such operations, to check fully every transaction and not to allow any waiter to leave until they are satisfied that all is in order.

Casual waiters often endeavour, sometimes successfully, to charge guests a higher price than that appearing on the list, earnestly hoping that their condition, perhaps at the close of the dinner, when they settle for all supplies, will be such that close scrutiny of the total charge will be waived.

Render your bill promptly and accurately, and be sure you send it to the correct person. See that every item is charged. Remember corkage. Sometimes you may be asked to add, say, ten per cent to the total for staff gratuities.

Prompt payment of these ensures the continued goodwill of
your staff. If you are sure the amount will be forthcoming
from the customer, add the gratuities at once to the sums
paid out to any jobbing staff. Regular staff can be paid
at the same time as they receive the first week's wages paid
after the event.

Provided due care is exercised it will be found that over
a long period the percentage of bad debts is infinitesimal.

CATERING FOR PARTICULAR FUNCTIONS

Dinners

These are popular and may possibly form the hard core
of this branch of your business. Those connected with
various associations and the like are mostly annual affairs,
and if satisfaction is given on the first occasion, it may well
become a permanent arrangement.

Assuming that your quotation has been accepted, the
menu and the date agreed, then acting on the estimate of
the anticipated numbers likely to be present, you can
proceed to plan. At least a week prior to the date fixed
provide your chef and head waiter (or manageress) with
detailed information as to: (*a*) name of association or
individual; (*b*) date and time of service; (*c*) menu chosen;
(*d*) table plan; (*e*) number of services required; and
(*f*) any special instructions. This will allow your chef to
make all his kitchen arrangements and to place orders for
the requisite food with the storeman and outside suppliers;
your head waiter to plan his staff, to arrange for supplies
of linen, china, glass and cutlery, to have all necessary
furniture cleaned and polished, and, having studied the
table plan, to arrange for seating and requisite service.
The manageress or housekeeper should arrange for the
supply of flowers and other decorations. The head waiter
or wine butler will make the necessary arrangements with
the cellarman or outside suppliers.

Trestle tables, their tops twenty-eight inches from floor level, should be used; they are easy to carry around and when not required can be folded and stacked away in comparatively small space. They should be set up according to the table plan, which is usually exhibited on an easel. Where a large number is expected the "comb" system should be used, a long table running from one end of the room to the other and having sprigs joining it every two yards, which will leave sufficient space for all service and allow guests to move about freely. Make certain that all tables are level and firm. Unless they are already covered with baize, soft cloths (worn tablecloths are useful) should be laid thereon, and then the top cloths with their centre creases running down the middle of each sprig, care being taken that patterns harmonize, so as to give the appearance of one long cloth. The space allotted to each guest—usually twenty-seven inches—should be sufficient to provide reasonable comfort and allow for efficient service. It is often the custom to have a name card placed on the table in front of each guest.

The collection of the dinner tickets may be made by your doorman on the arrival of the guests, or at the tables just before coffee is served. Whichever method is adopted always agree with the secretary or organizer the exact number present. It is imperative when making up your bill and obviates disputes.

It is usual for guests to assemble in a separate room, in which cocktails and apéritifs are served before the meal. The arrangements for this are made by the head waiter. The bar can be constructed of one or two trestle tables mounted on beer cases, all being fully covered by a buffet cloth. There should be a few small lounge tables, on which are placed ashtrays and *raviers* of potato crisps, cheese straws, olives and salted almonds.

If there is no toastmaster this duty is performed by the head waiter. At formal dinners it is usual for the head waiter, when announcing that dinner is served, to name those sitting at the top table; on less ceremonial occasions this may be dispensed with.

When all guests have been comfortably seated and grace (often omitted) has been said, the service can commence. The head waiter or whoever may be supervising should always give the signal to begin serving each course and to clear the used plates afterwards. The waiter serving the top table is the first to begin, all other waiters taking their time from him. Service at the top table begins with the chairman, then the guest on his right, then the guest on his left, and then along the whole table.

Waiters have from eight to ten covers according to the menu and the importance of the dinner. Wine waiters have from twenty to thirty guests each. Service should flow evenly from kitchen to service-room and then to the dining-room.

After the service of the last course, and prior to the service of coffee, all cruets, sugar-sifters, table-napkins and unused cutlery must be removed. Coffee-cups, saucers and plates should then be placed before the guests, along with sugar-bowls and a plentiful supply of ashtrays. Before the service of coffee the loyal toast should be proposed by the chairman. Coffee is then served and guests may smoke. Then follow the usual speeches in response to the toasts, interspersed as often as not by songs and musical items. The only staff who should remain in the room are the wine butler and wine waiters.

Unless wine is inclusive in the price of the dinner ticket, and this is not usual in these times, it is the duty of the wine waiters to obtain payment from guests for all liquor supplied, either at the time of service or at the end of the evening, if the guest so desires. When taking orders at the tables wine waiters should write out chits in duplicate, handing the top copies to the barman, who will price them. The waiter will pay from his float for all supplies obtained, recouping himself from the guests. At the top table the chairman usually acts as host and settles his bill at the close of the evening. Credit must never be given, and all wine waiters should be made personally responsible for all wine, etc., supplied to them from the bar.

A point to watch is what happens to portions of food left over. If preparations have been made for two hundred guests and only one hundred and eighty-seven sit down, the balance of thirteen dinners is valuable and some at least can be made up for the following day's business.

Dinner Dances

Here two activities, so to speak, are combined. The procedure is either: (*a*) reception, dinner, dance with a light running buffet; or (*b*) reception, dancing, dinner, more dancing. Three rooms may be required: reception, dancing and dinner. After the service of the meal the dining-room can be converted into the buffet.

The reception is similar to that preceding a dinner, while the meal, whenever it may be served, is usually less formal than in the case of a dinner only. For example, instead of sprigs there may be separate tables arranged to accommodate eight, ten, twelve or fourteen guests. The meal itself is also less elaborate, the speeches fewer in number and decidedly brief, thus leaving time for dancing.

The running buffet should be of a light nature, consisting of tea, coffee, soft drinks, pastries and ices. The length of the buffet table will depend upon the number of guests. It should be set up at the end of the room, or alternatively down part of one side, whichever is more convenient for service. It can be built up in the same manner as the bar referred to in the previous section, with all refreshments set out in an appetizing manner. Have some small tables around, with ashtrays, sugar and milk. The buffet tables should be tastefully dressed with flowers.

Should alcoholic drinks be available it will be necessary

to erect a bar, which can either be in the same room as the buffet or in a separate room. If the function is a private one it will fall upon the host or hostess to offer hospitality, but if it is a more or less public affair drinks should be paid for as ordered, either from the waiters or, if the guests obtain direct service, at the bar.

Frequently the caterer is asked to arrange for the services of a dance band. This done, remember to provide a supper for the band, and ascertain if liquid refreshments are to be made available for them. Request the leader to submit a dance programme, which should be sent to either the host or to the secretary/organizer for approval. On occasions the caterer will be asked to supply balloons, paper hats, streamers, etc., which will form an extra charge.

At the close of the dance it is customary, particularly at a private function, to serve small cups of hot clear soup to all the guests on leaving.

Make absolutely certain of the exact numbers present.

Dances

These may be either private or connected with some club or association. Important points are date, expected numbers, duration, and style of buffet desired. Two rooms are essential—ballroom and buffet room, which may include the bar. Success of a dance is measured by dance band, floor and buffet, in that order. Make sure that the ballroom floor is perfect.

The buffet should be arranged in the same manner as set out above, but is, of course, more elaborate: tea, coffee, soft drinks, various sandwiches, pastries, savouries, creams, jellies, fruit salad, and ices. On each table set around the room should be placed sugar-bowl, milk and ashtrays. Assuming the period of the dance to be from 8 p.m. till 1 a.m., the buffet service should be made available from 9 p.m. till 12.30 a.m. Make sure you have ample staff on duty, especially at the opening hour of the buffet, when pressure is heaviest. Later on a smaller staff normally suffices.

All points already set out relating to the band, etc., apply.

Ball Suppers

These are similar to the dances described in the previous section, except that a set supper is served, usually shortly after midnight. The menu depends upon the price charged. Generally, however, the dishes are so adapted as to be easy to serve. Tables may be arranged in " comb " formation, but it is more usual to have round and square tables seating from four to sixteen persons.

It is advisable to have plenty of waiters on duty, as frequently many changes take place, guests arranging parties during the evening, and the setting up must be elastic. When large numbers are involved, supper is often served in relays. In some instances there may be a light buffet available.

As ball suppers frequently run on till 4 a.m. and even to 5 a.m., breakfast is often served just prior to the finish, this consisting of tea, coffee, toast, bacon and eggs, sausages and kippers. Naturally, well-equipped bars are most essential. Rapid service all round is imperative.

Wedding Receptions

These require very special attention, chiefly because it is the day of days for the bride and her mother. In most cases such receptions will prove a most excellent free advertisement for you and should be productive of future business.

The function can be: (a) reception; (b) reception and breakfast; (c) reception and luncheon. Where the number of guests is very large a reception only is advisable. The setting out is similar to that for a dance buffet: tables with spotless white cloths, plenty of flowers, white being predominant, foliage and smilax; refreshments consisting of tea, coffee, fruit cup, various sandwiches, pastries, slab cake, *petit fours*, jellies, creams and ices. Arrangements are usually made for sherry and/or champagne to be handed round when the toast of the bride and bridegroom is proposed. See that there are a number of small tables available, and chairs for those who desire to sit, such as the elderly folk.

At very fashionable wedding receptions the waiters should wear with the usual dress coats white waistcoats, white ties and white gloves; the head waiter his normal dress clothes, a black tie and no gloves. When the wedding presents are on display a commissionaire or private detective should be engaged to keep an eye on them and also on the guests perhaps.

It is customary for all the guests to be announced by the head waiter. They are received (usually) by the bride's parents, and then shake hands with the bride and bridegroom. Thereafter the food and liquid refreshments are served by the waiting staff, many of the guests assisting as a rule. After these refreshments the wedding cake is cut, a large knife with a white or silver handle being used. A large wedge is usually cut beforehand in the cake. At the appropriate moment the head waiter goes forward and removes the vase of flowers set on top, the tiers and the supporting pillars, leaving the bottom tier only. He then hands the knife to the bride, who is assisted by the bridegroom in cutting the cake, which is really only making an incision. The cake is then removed to a side table, where it is cut into small finger lengths, each having icing and marzipan, placed on silver trays or baskets, and handed round to the guests, small plates and cake knives and forks being provided.

At this moment glasses of sherry and/or champagne are passed round, and the toast of the happy couple proposed, usually by the clergyman, or an uncle or near relative of the bride. Congratulatory telegrams are usually read by the best man.

As the reception nears its end the bride and bridegroom make preparations for leaving. Here it is essential to provide separate rooms for changing into their going-away apparel. The guests all assemble and speed the couple on their way with good wishes, much cheering and hilarity, accompanied by showers of confetti, rose leaves and streamers. On occasion an old horseshoe or an empty can is tied to the back of the car for luck.

Each lady guest usually receives on leaving a piece of the wedding cake in a small, coloured paper bag. The caterer is often asked to provide and address boxes for posting pieces of cake to those who may have sent presents and not attended the celebrations. Inserted with the cake is a small card printed in silver, bearing the name of the bride before marriage, her married name and the address of the couple's future home.

Where a wedding breakfast or luncheon is desired the table setting is dictated by the menu, arrangements being a matter for the host and hostess to decide. It is customary to have a top table at which will be seated the clergyman, bride and bridegroom, best man, bridesmaids, the parents, and sometimes very near relatives. The remaining guests will be seated at sprigs or separate tables. If desired the menu can be printed in silver on dainty cards, which are often kept as souvenirs. The bride's bouquet should be placed in front of her. All tables should have ample flowers.

It is usual for a reception-room to be made available. Here the guests can assemble before proceeding to the banquet room. Cocktails are frequently served. A table plan should be placed on an easel, or the seating arrangements announced by the head waiter table by table, these being numbered. Place cards are set out on the tables.

By Scottish law, marriages can be solemnized by an

ordained clergyman not only in a church, as in England, but also almost anywhere else, the only condition being that the prospective bride and bridegroom must have the intimation of their intention to marry made in the church of the parish in which they reside. This is known as " calling the banns ".

It follows, then, that in Scotland the caterer is frequently asked to provide accommodation and make all the necessary arrangements for the actual ceremony, which can be held in the morning, afternoon or evening. The last is extremely popular, as it relieves guests, especially men, of the necessity to ask for leave of absence from business.

A room must be provided with a small dais or platform from which the officiating clergyman will conduct the service, the couple standing or kneeling before him. Chairs are placed in rows for the guests, a centre passage being left. The front row on either side is set apart for the parents and close relatives of the couple. Hymn-sheets are provided by the caterer. They can be kept in stock and should have the usual well-known hymns appropriate to a wedding printed thereon in silver. A pianist is required to accompany the singing and to play the " Wedding March ".

Upon completion of the ceremony the bride and bridegroom walk slowly down the centre passage. They are followed by the clergyman, bridesmaids, best man and the parents into a separate room, where intimate congratulations are offered and the marriage certificate completed. The reception then follows, either in the same room or in an adjoining one.

The photographing of the wedding party after the ceremony is arranged by the caterer as a general rule.

Whist Drives and Bridge Drives

Because they have many points in common these two can be treated here as one. They may be held in the afternoon (ladies only) or in the evening, which is more popular. In the room set apart for the playing should be card tables, packs of cards, scoring cards, pencils, ashtrays, book matches, and sometimes cigarettes and dishes of sweets.

At a suitable moment play is suspended and an adjournment made to another room for the service of refreshments of a light nature: tea and coffee (the latter an evening beverage), sandwiches, savouries, pastries, fruit salad and ices.

A table is usually provided for display of prizes.

Suppers

These are somewhat informal affairs run by sports clubs. The menu is simple, and the seating is top table with sprigs. Speeches are or should be of a lively nature and interspersed with musical items. Bar facilities should be available all the evening. Beer is the most popular drink.

Twenty-first Birthday Parties

These resemble wedding receptions in that they are one of the high-lights in the lives of young people. A call on the caterer is made by the parents or guardians, and the ensuing evening proceedings consist of a reception, some dancing, then a set supper or maybe a buffet, followed by more dancing.

The arriving guests are received by the host and hostess and by the young lady or gentleman who is celebrating her or his majority. To occupy the guests, most of whom will be young, the dancing should commence at once. Later a break is made for the service of the supper or opening of the buffet. The supper menu may consist of *hors d'œuvres* or soup, fish, meat course, sweet and coffee, while the buffet would be of a nature similar to that for an ordinary dance. At the conclusion of the supper or first service at the buffet a birthday cake is brought in and duly cut by the young host or hostess. Thereafter small pieces are handed round along with such liquid refreshment as is in accord with the desires of the host and the average age of the guests.

A near relative then proposes the toast, and all join in singing the ever-popular song, " I'm twenty-one to-day ". A large key made of gilt-coloured cardboard is then presented. Speeches should be few and short. Dancing is shortly resumed and, if desired, the service of a buffet made available. When this follows a supper it is of a light nature.

Cocktail Parties

It is possible that you will be asked to provide for these. The essential is a well-stocked bar, tastefully set up, numbers of tables and chairs, and plenty of ashtrays. Despite the fact that it is called a cocktail party the drinks served are rather varied, and it is advisable to have a wide selection available. Provide dishes of potato crisps, olives, *canapés*, etc.

Breakfasts

Occasion may arise when you may be asked to provide such a meal. If it is to be a full English breakfast it should include: choice of orange juice, grapefruit or melon; porridge or cereal with cream; main dish of bacon and eggs, finnon haddock, fried fillets of sole or plaice, or sausage and egg; tea and coffee; toast, rolls, butter, marmalade and jam.

The table set-up depends upon the desire of the patron, but if it is a business organization it is likely to be a top table with the usual sprigs.

Silver and Golden Weddings

The celebrations consist, for the most part, of a reception followed by a dinner. The cake (if any) has silver or golden decorations, according to whether it is to mark twenty-five or fifty years of married bliss, and is served with the wine at the reception.

Speeches figure largely at the dinners and are often long-winded, being of a reminiscent nature. Any congratulatory telegrams received are read by someone at the top table. After the meal there may be a short dance, but this is contingent upon the number and ages of the guests.

Exhibitions

These will include trade shows, accommodation being provided for the display of furniture, radios, television sets, etc., in one or a number of rooms. As visitors are usually by trade invitation, some form of hospitality is essential. A bar is erected for the service of cocktails, beer, spirits, etc., and a buffet table for the service of sandwiches, tea and coffee. In the winter months small bowls of soup are welcome.

OUTSIDE CATERING

Outside catering presents a number of problems that often require the exercise of considerable ingenuity before they can be overcome. The rate of wastage is high, so there must be sufficient supplies of linen, silver, cutlery, china and glass, as well as collapsible tables and chairs to meet requirements. Unless the occasion is a special one, china, glass and cutlery can be of a tougher variety than is normally used in a fixed establishment. Transport from your own place to the venue is another factor to be considered. If you are contemplating doing this type of business on a fairly large scale, you should endeavour to have your own transport, driver and basic staff. This will ensure much more careful handling of stock, and also reduce running costs.

Additional staff—waiters, waitresses, chefs and serving

staff, including washers-up and porters—can be recruited from lists kept at your office of those who are suitable and willing to undertake this type of work, which is termed jobbing. The number and type of staff required is determined by the nature of the function, number of guests expected, length of time of service—e.g., whether a reception, dinner or dinner dance—and also by the facilities or lack of them in the particular building.

Payment of staff is usually at a fixed rate per hour, dependent on grade. Alternatively it may be a fixed sum— for example, fifteen shillings for setting up, serving and clearing a dinner. Settlement is made immediately the service is completed. National insurance contribution is deducted if the card has not already been stamped by a previous employer in that week.

Care must be taken when framing estimates for these functions, for several expenses must be included that do not come into the total figure pertaining to a function held in your own premises. Among these are: (a) high rate of breakages and wastage; (b) cost of hiring any additional plant or equipment; (c) transport charges, whether outside contractors or by your own vehicles; (d) charges for gas, electricity, water, gratuities to caretakers, porters, etc.; (e) cost of any licences.

Mention must be made of the opportunities offered to provide catering facilities in the private homes of local residents. Here working conditions are usually good, and the risk of wastage, etc., is much lower. Revenue can also be obtained by hiring out such equipment as tables, chairs, linen, cutlery, china and glass to private householders. An important point here is that a most accurate record must be kept of all articles lent on hire, the charges to be made and the arrangements for collection. Charges should include all breakages, losses and other damage done to your property.

A final word on functions as a whole. They are a grand

and cheap form of advertisement, bringing to your establishment many persons who may never have visited it before. Provided you make a good impression, you can be certain that they will bring to you any business they have, whether it be function trade or just patronizing your restaurant for a meal. Always bear in mind that every function is extremely important not only to the host, the hostess or the organizer, but also to you.

INDEX